To

Jean + Cliff

I really appreciate ... too!

In His ...

Ray

GOD'S WAY TO A MORE PERFECT YOU

Living by the Fruit of the Spirit!

GOD'S WAY TO A
MORE PERFECT YOU

Living by the Fruit of the Spirit!

LEROY LAWSON

COLLEGE PRESS
PUBLISHING COMPANY
Joplin, Missouri

Library of Congress Catalog Card Number: 92-75788
International Standard Book Number:0-89900-610-8

TABLE OF CONTENTS ❧

INTRODUCTION ❧

GOD'S WAY TO A MORE PERFECT YOU

Your high school English teacher wouldn't approve of the "more perfect" in the title. "More perfect" is like "more better" – tolerable when uttered by a three-year-old, but hardly appropriate for a literate speaker or writer. Besides, the good instructor would insist, something is either perfect or not perfect; there aren't gradations of perfection. The definition, you'll recall, is "without defect, blemish, or any imperfection." Colloquial English often cheats, of course, but in the classroom – and in the title of a serious book – we should be precise. Perfect, if you please.

You could also protest the title hints of little serious Bible study and much Madison Avenue propaganda. If you did, I'd have to plead guilty. That's why I chose it. I'm borrowing advertising's language to lure you to listen to God's Good News. These days all sorts of glitzy ads bombard us, guaranteeing a"transformed you" with the purchase of this or that expensively priced elixir. A more wonderful – if not a "more perfect" – you can be yours for the buying.

Years ago I studied in a holiness college which required a course in "The Doctrine of Holiness." A kindly little old lady (who was probably about the age I am now) was the instructor. One day as Miss Shipley was trying her best to explain the doctrine of the "second blessing," she assured us that, when and if we received this second act of grace from God, we would then be perfect. She didn't mean perfectly perfect, she wanted us to know, but relatively perfect.

As a young and brash English major more at home with the vagaries of language than the obscurities of theology, I raised my hand. "Miss Shipley," I submitted, as politely as I could, "I'm having difficulty understanding this doctrine. It seems to me that something is either perfect or imperfect. There aren't degrees of perfection, since being perfect means being complete or whole. Something that isn't perfect is imperfect. It can't be more or less perfect." (Straight out of my high school English class.)

The patient Miss Shipley, who had entertained my questions before, sighed. "I'm certain, Mr. Lawson, that if you will just go home and pray about it, you'll understand." Thus did the good lady dodge the question. By this point in the course Miss Shipley was repairing to prayer on my behalf with increasing frequency.

Well, I prayed and it still didn't make sense to me. Do we

attain absolute perfection with this "second blessing"? If we do, why do some of its propagandists appear not to have received it, at least when judged by their conduct? The fault I find in the doctrine must be charged to the vocabulary, not the experience.

Equally disturbing are popular dogmas contending for humanity's inherent goodness, even perfection. (Do they seriously think this is as good as we can get? A frightening prospect.) What we are is what human beings are supposed to be, they claim. You're OK and I'm OK. It's a dangerous deception. I'm convinced, to the contrary, that you're not OK and I'm not OK but that's OK because God is OK and he's made a way for us to become OK through Jesus Christ.

My title, then, starts where the humanists (and most Americans, whatever their professed religion) are and goes beyond them. So that we can start at the same place, I'm accepting that we are, humanly speaking, perfect. But if I have to use the term, then I have to go against the dictates of my excellent English instructor and insist, "We ought to be, we can be, even more perfect."

As far as Jesus is concerned, the standard is absolute:

Be perfect, therefore, as your heavenly Father is perfect. (Matt 5:48).

In the Sermon on the Mount, Jesus is trying to change his disciples' method of dealing with their enemies. He prescribes love and prayer and returning good for evil. He proscribes vengeance. Godliness (acting like God) is required to mend broken relationships.

It would be far easier to be a humanist, with no supernatural standard to attain. If godliness is the ideal for perfect human behavior, then who could dare claim to be truly OK? If one has already dismissed God from the universe, then he can perhaps profess a certain kind of human superiority. The Christian is at a disadvantage here. Having met Jesus, he can boast no more. He has seen the best, and he isn't it. Not only has he lost his right to brag of his OKness, he has also lost his complacency. Having glimpsed perfection, he desires it for himself, even though he knows he cannot attain it on his own. He needs divine assistance.

That assistance is available through the kind offices of the Holy Spirit, by whose aid growth to full spiritual maturity is achieved. The fruit of the Spirit's impact on our lives is the subject of this book. I make this blunt statement of my thesis before I get into the body of the book, because in the succeeding chapters you may wonder whether I have forgotten or perhaps don't even know the marks of spirituality. You may be disappointed to learn, for example, that such topics as speaking in tongues or experiencing miracles or signs won't be treated; neither will suggestions for improving your prayers and enhancing your Bible study. Instead, the book is about developing a responsible character, attaining emotional maturity, and having an "attitude . . . the same as that of Christ Jesus" (Phil 2:5). These are the goals of the quest for personal completeness. They require what the Apostle Paul calls "the fruit of the Spirit."

Galatians 5:22 and 23 provide the outline for the book. The preceding verses are a convincing argument for a life lived in the power of the Holy Spirit.

> You, my brothers, were called to be free. But do not use your freedom to indulge the sinful nature; rather, serve one another

in love. The entire law is summed up in a single command, "Love your neighbor as yourself." If you keep on biting and devouring each other, watch out or you will be destroyed by each other.

So I say, live by the Spirit, and you will not gratify the desires of the sinful nature. For the sinful nature desires what is contrary to the Spirit, and the Spirit what is contrary to the sinful nature. They are in conflict with each other, so that you do not do what you want. But if you are led by the Spirit, you are not under law.

The acts of the sinful nature are obvious: sexual immorality, impurity and debauchery; idolatry and witchcraft; hatred, discord, jealousy, fits of rage, selfish ambition, dissensions, factions and envy; drunkenness, orgies, and the like. I warn you, as I did before, that those who live like this will not inherit the kingdom of God.

But the fruit of the Spirit is love, joy, peace, patience, kindness, goodness, faithfulness, gentleness and self-control. Against such things there is no law. Those who belong to Christ Jesus have crucified the sinful nature with its passions and desires. Since we live by the Spirit, let us keep in step with the Spirit. Let us not become conceited, provoking and envying each other (Gal 5:13-26).

PREMISE: YOU ARE FREE

You are free in Christ, Paul argues throughout the Galatian letter, while at the same time warning against equating that freedom with self-indulgence, since to do so is to invite self-destruction. The rare, remarkable freedom in Christ grants us the liberty to love ("Serve one another in love") with an uncoerced and responsible love.

Where such responsibility is missing, so is maturity. One does not reach full adulthood until willing to accept full liability for one's actions. We call an irresponsible person "childish." Emil Brunner goes so far as to equate true responsibility with

11

true humanity, to be achieved by a scriptural response to God:

> If any human being were ever to respond to God in harmony
> with His Word, and upon the basis of His word, in believing
> love, he would be truly human.[1]

"Spiritual life" is whatever it takes to become truly human, to
reach our highest God-given potential, to rise above the masses
of men and women who seem merely to exist for the moment
without thought of eternity or excellence. Believing as we do
that freedom is the prerequisite to self-improvement, we unfortunately defeat ourselves by misunderstanding (either innocently
or deliberately) that freedom does not mean the absence of any
restraints. It is that misunderstanding that the Apostle Paul is at
such pains to correct in this passage.

OPTIONS: WHICH WILL YOU CHOOSE ?

Will you satisfy your sinful nature?

"The acts of the sinful nature are obvious," Paul declares,
then offers a catalog complete enough to include our favorite
ones. You may be innocent of sexual immorality or debauchery, for example, or even idolatry or witchcraft. But what about
hatred? Are you ever given to spreading discord or entertaining
jealousy or envy or rage? Are you ambitious? For yourself, or
another?

Who can read Paul's list without squirming? Who hasn't
yearned sometime, maybe often, to run away and start over
again, in the hope of doing better next time?

That desire to escape is a hopeful sign. As George MacDonald has so wisely observed, "A beast does not know that he is a beast, and the nearer a man gets to being a beast the less he knows."[2] The thoroughly debauched deny their state. The hardened sinner protests his innocence. Paradoxically, the spiritual are painfully aware of their sinfulness.

Kim Hubbard quipped somewhere, "The reason the way of the transgressor is so hard is that it's so crowded." In the beginning, though, the transgressor's way seems infinitely easier than the way of the cross. He's just doing what comes naturally. He's one of the crowd. The beginning of the sinner's career is a breeze; it's the end that's so painful. You can count on it. Self-indulgence can lead to only one conclusion: biting and devouring one other.

Look at the list again. The works of the sinful nature are anti-relational. Dedicate yourself to yourself, look out first and always for Number One, and see how well you get along with other people. You won't; you'll be too busy fighting for your rights, insisting on your way, doing your thing and doing it your way, to even think about, let alone act lovingly toward, anyone else. You'll probably get what you want, but your petty victories can't buy you happiness.

My experience agrees with Chuck Swindoll's. Speaking of former Christians who have renounced their life in the Spirit for one of the flesh, he says, "I've never seen a genuinely joyful backslidden Christian in my life. Never! I've never met one who could look me straight in the eye and say these are the happiest years of my life."[3] It's no wonder, though, is it? The kind of happiness Swindoll is talking about has to do with relationships with God and other people. Insist on being your own god, and you alone must make you happy.

In Jeremiah 2 the Lord questions an entire backslidden nation.

My people have committed two sins:
They have forsaken me,
the spring of living water,
and have dug their own cisterns,
broken cisterns that cannot hold water.
Is Israel a servant, a slave by birth?
Why then has he become plunder?
Lions have roared;
they have growled at him.
They have laid waste his land; his towns are burned and desert-
ed. (13-15)

The answer to the first question is *no*. God's people were not designed to be slaves.

The second question is easily answered. The nation suffers at the hands of others because the people thought they could do things better than God. They even manufactured inferior wells, preferring their cobbled cisterns to God's reliable springs. Verse 17 summarizes God's judgment:

Have you not brought this on yourselves
by forsaking the Lord your God
when he led you in the way?

You had to do it your way. You knew better than I did. You declared your freedom from me – and forged your own destruction.

Are you satisfied?

Will you satisfy your spiritual nature?

The life of the "sinful nature" (or "the flesh," as older versions translate the Greek *sarx*), and "life in the spirit" are as different as society and solitude. In the one, the individual always comes first. In the other, relationships rule, and wherever two

14

or more persons are primarily concerned about strengthening the ties that bind them, laws to protect them from each other are unnecessary.

We'll be devoting one chapter to each item mentioned in the fruit of the Spirit. We'll waste no time reading laws (religious, civic, national, or otherwise) which authorities have passed against "love, joy, peace, patience, kindness, goodness, faithfulness, gentleness and self-control." To the contrary, "against such things there is no law."

Of course not. Can you imagine passing a law against love? What elected official would introduce legislation against joy? Who would ever openly issue a proclamation against peace? (Even when war is declared, it is to preserve the peace, they say.) If there were a law against patience, I'd be a model, law-abiding citizen! You wouldn't propose a law deliberately banning kindness, would you? Or goodness? Or faithfulness, gentleness, and self-control? The questions are absurd.

The fruit of the Spirit, then, enables persons to live together in harmony. Is it any wonder that devout Christians by and large make such good citizens? They're not angry, bitter or upset all the time. They demand fewer rights – but will work harder for other people's – than their counterparts. A nation of Spirit-abiding Christians would be a poor place in which to practice law. Citizens there would be an energetic group, however, since so little of their emotional energy would be expended on destructive emotions and actions. Spontaneity would mark their behavior; since they would have no need to hold themselves in check.

Flannery O'Connor captures the essence of this quality in her phrase, "the special super-aliveness that holiness is."[4] Miss O'Connor's insight differs drastically from most people's tainted view of sanctity. "Super-aliveness" hardly comes to mind when someone is called a saint, does it? "Holiness" or "saintliness" is rather the achievement of people too old and too tired to get into trouble. They couldn't have been holy when they were young; they had too much energy then! Now grown too feeble to sin enthusiastically, they have turned their attention to more spiritual things. (Who has ever heard of a blonde or brunette or muscular saint? Aren't they always gray-haired?)

Miss O'Connor's right, though, isn't she? You've known them, holy persons in every age bracket, who walk by the Spirit. You just haven't thought to call them saints – they seem to be having too much fun for "spiritual" persons. You can tell it by their joy, their curiosity, their vitality, yes, their "super-aliveness."

Van Wick Brooks has another phrase I'd like to borrow here. He is not speaking specifically about Christians when he writes of these "magnanimous people," but what he describes is always a goal for those who live in the Spirit:

How delightful is the company of generous people, who overlook trifles and keep their minds instinctively fixed on whatever is good and positive in the world about them. People of small caliber are always carping. They are bent on showing their own superiority, their knowledge or prowess or good breeding. But magnanimous people have no vanity, they have no jealousy, they have no reserves and they feed on the true and the solid wherever they find it and what is more, they find it everywhere.[5]

They are super-alive.

THE STRUGGLE IS REAL

As Paul contrasts the two options, you'd think the choice would be simple. But as anyone who has ever tried to live up to his own standards (let alone the Lord's) can testify, temptation is an ever-present companion.

In a famous passage even Paul, years after his conversion, writes of his contest as if it were always present,

> I do not understand what I do. For what I want to do I do not do, but what I hate I do. . . . For I have the desire to do what is good, but I cannot carry it out. For what I do is not the good I want to do; no, the evil I do not want to do – this I keep on doing (Rom 7:15-19).

Who doesn't? Scholars debate whether Paul is describing himself as he was before fully yielding to Christ and to the Spirit or after. I suspect it doesn't matter. Even after, we are pretty helpless on our own to resist the lure to do wrong. "What a wretched man I am!" Paul cries out. But he is not alone and he is not helpless. "Thanks be to God – through Jesus Christ our Lord!" The contest is real, but so is the presence of Christ's Spirit in the midst of the contest. We can win, if we really want to live in the Spirit.

If we want to. Did you read Stevenson's *Dr. Jekyll and Mr. Hyde* when you were young? It is one of those stories ("with a good moral," our parents were wont to say) that helped frame our youthful understanding of sin. The good young scientist Dr. Jekyll experiments with a psyche-altering drug and is startled to discover the power of evil growing in him. Under the drug's influence his alter ego, Mr. Hyde, takes over. At first Jekyll has to work to overcome his moral inhibitions in order to enter fully into Mr. Hyde's world, but he succeeds. He eases deeper and deeper into the role, in time dedicating his evenings to sensuality. He realizes he is gradually losing hold of his original and better self, but he is having too much fun to stop.

The time comes for him to decide once and for all which personality will prevail. If he chooses to be Dr. Jekyll, he'll have to give up his sensual pleasures; if Edward Hyde, he will lose the better aspirations and high principles to which he has long devoted himself. And he will die despised and friendless. At last he casts his lot with Dr. Jekyll, only to discover his strength is gone. To his horror, he can't return to his better life. He thinks he is through with evil, but evil is not through with him.

You may be through with drink, but drink isn't through with you.

You may be through with promiscuity, but promiscuity isn't through with you.

You may be through with drugs, but drugs aren't through with you.

You may be through with dangerous eating habits, but they aren't through with you.

Anyone who has ever battled addiction understands Jekyll's predicament. You can't break it by yourself. Sinful nature can't cure itself. That's what makes life in the Spirit so essential.

THE OUTCOME IS PREDICTABLE

That wonderful preacher Peter Marshall loved to tell stories of his homeland, Scotland. A favorite was about a Scottish lad in Aberdeen whose mother was a strict disciplinarian. She regularly corrected the little boy with one of two sentences. "Now God won't like that," she would reprove him. When he was being especially bad, she'd announce, "God will be angry."

Her method worked pretty well most of the time, but it didn't work the night she served prunes for dessert (prunes being the Scottish boy's equivalent of an American boy's broccoli). The lad wouldn't eat them, so his mother applied both sentences. "Now God won't like this." She was convinced He looked with divine displeasure on little boys who won't finish their prunes. "God will be angry," she scolded, but he wouldn't budge. Chastising him once more for his naughtiness, she sent him off to bed.

That night a terrible thunderstorm arose. As it banged and crashed about, the mother worried about her little lad having to endure the storm alone in his room. She went upstairs and opened his door, expecting to find him cowering in his bed, but he wasn't there. Instead he was at the window, studying the sights. When he heard his mother come in, he said, "My, my, sic a fuss to mak ower twa prunes."[6]

Some church members listen to their preacher thundering against the acts of a sinful nature and walk away muttering, "My, my such a fuss to make over a little sin." But thunder he must, because what seems so insignificant if left unattended will grow, like Dr. Jekyll's obsession, into Mr. Hyde's overpowering domination.

Remember *Alice in Wonderland*, when Alice meets the Cheshire cat? She asks, "Cheshire-Puss . . . would you tell me please, which way I ought to go from here?"

"That depends a good deal on where you want to get to."

Alice begins to answer, "I don't much care where . . . " but the Cheshire-Puss interrupts. "Well, then it doesn't matter which way you go."

Alice adds, "So long as I get somewhere."

And the cat says, "Oh, you're sure to do that. If you only walk long enough, you'll get somewhere."

So we set out in life, not much caring where we went, so long as it was somewhere. Mostly we were interested in whether we could have a good time along the way. And we enjoyed. Then one morning we woke up middle-aged. We'd arrived somewhere. But it wasn't what we had in mind at all. We'd wasted forty years and we couldn't go back and start over.

None of us started the journey in our youth by vowing, "What I really want to do is lead a life of biting and devouring and destroying other people. That's what I really want to do." No. We didn't look ahead, didn't consider consequences, but just let nature take its course. We didn't consider our lifestyles' sinful nature; that's what got us into trouble.

And that's why preachers make such a fuss over a little sin.

And why this preacher hopes you understand you only have two options. You can do what comes naturally, and pay the price.

Or you can live life in the Spirit, and reap the reward.

FOR YOUR FURTHER CONSIDERATION

1. Why is the author so hard on thinking, "You're OK and I'm OK?" Do you agree or disagree with him? What does the Bible teach about OKness?

2. What is the basic difference between a humanist and a Christian?

3. How do you define spirituality? How does the author? How does the Bible?

4. Emil Brunner equates true responsibility with true humanity. What do you think it means to be truly human?

5. Read again the list of characteristics of the sinful nature. Do you find yourself anywhere in the list? If so, how can you get off of it?

6. Why does the author say "the works of the sinful nature are anti-relational"? What does he mean?

7. Do think that having the fruit of the Spirit will make a person, to borrow Flannery O'Connor's term, "super-alive"?

8. Do you know anyone who has had an experience similar to Dr. Jekyll's? What happened?

9. At the conclusion of the chapter, two options for life are presented. What are they? What are the consequences of each?

Endnotes

1. Emil Brunner, *Man in Revolt*. pp. 51, 53.
2. *George MacDonald, An Anthology*, ed. C. S. Lewis. London: Fount Paperbacks, 1946, p. 141.
3. Charles Swindoll, *Three Steps Forward, Two Steps Back*. Bantam Books, 1980, p. 180.
4. *The Habit of Being, Letters of Flannery O'Connor*, ed. Sally Fitzgerald. New York: Vintage Books, 1979, p. 280.
5. Van Wick Brooks, *A Chilmark Miscellany*. New York: E. P. Dutton and Company, Inc., 1948, p. 6.
6. Catherine Marshall, *A Man Called Peter*. New York, et al.: McGraw-Hill Book Company, 1951, pp. 156, 157.

LOVE 🕊

"The fruit of the Spirit is *Love* . . . ."

The traveling executive was nursing his bedtime drink in the hotel bar when a friendly, attractive woman caught his eye. She accepted his offer to treat her to one. Then another. The conversation went smoothly; she found him amusing. He found it easy to invite her to his room; she found it easy to accept. He was far from home and lonely. A little loving was just the thing he needed. She was willing.

Afterwards he slept soundly. When he woke up, she was already gone, but he saw the note she left him, scrawled in bright red lipstick across the dresser mirror. "Welcome to the wonderful world of AIDS."[1]

This was not what he had bargained for. He'd just been looking for a good time, a little sexual gratification, what our society mistakenly calls "making love." Instead he bought disease.

He learned a bitter lesson. Love is not sex; it is not lust. Neither is it "going for the gusto," nor keeping "a little thing going on the side." "Having sex" (another misleading expression) is not "making love." Sometimes, as the executive learned to his dismay, it is making hate. This woman would die shortly, probably condemned by love-making. She was getting even by taking out her hatred on the man or men who did her wrong.

She helps us define our problem as we begin this study, doesn't she? How can something as pleasurable as making love turn out so bad? What is "love," anyway, that the same word is used to explain what Christ was doing on the cross *for* humanity and what the woman was doing in bed *against* humanity? What are we to understand when we read that "the fruit of the Spirit is *love?*"

Should we even use the term? Would we be better off substituting something else, like compassion or affection or charity? Maybe we should take Ralph Sockman's advice and give *love* a rest.[2] Although he calls it "the identifying mark of a Christian," he complains that "love is an overworked word for an unemployed emotion" and urges us to stop "this profanation of our most sacred common noun." While agreeing the word *love* is too much with us even though the real thing is not, we'll not take up Sockman's cause. It's not so much our abuse of the word that offends as the rarity of the thing itself. Without the spiritual nutrient called love we wither and die. Possessing it, we not only are blessed but we become the conduit of blessings to others.

Everybody familiar with the Christian faith knows Jesus commanded his disciples to love one another. But knowing isn't doing, is it? What is difficult about the love Jesus demonstrates, as opposed to the love we make, is his treating it as a command to be obeyed rather than as a feeling to be enjoyed.

A new commandment I give you: love one another. As I have loved you, so you must love one another. All men will know that you are my disciples if you love one another (John 13:34, 35).

Feelings can't be commanded; actions can. Sockman says love is an unemployed emotion. He restricts it too much. Emotion is involved, to be sure, but love is something far more comprehensive. To love as Christ loved calls for consecrated emotions, intelligence, motives, and actions. Only such a virtue can be patient, kind, lacking in envy, humble, courteous, quick to serve, slow to become angry, forgetful of slights suffered, delighting in truth, protective, trusting, hopeful, persevering, and completely dependable (1 Cor 13:4-8).

LOVE DEFINED:
JESUS CHRIST LAID DOWN HIS LIFE FOR US
1 JOHN 3:16

"The fruit of the spirit is love," Paul writes, and we nod approvingly. We like love. We sing about it, talk about it, dream about it, and yearn for more of it – until we realize what Jesus meant by that little clause, "as I have loved you." John makes Jesus' meaning clear with a directness that leaves us squirming:

This is how God showed his love among us: He sent his one

and only Son into the world that we might live through him. This is love: not that we loved God, but that he loved us and sent his Son as an atoning sacrifice for our sins (1 John 4:9, 10).

It's the word *sacrifice* that wakes us out of our complacency. Love is costly; it demands the ultimate. A person can't do any more than Jesus did for us – and nothing less is acceptable.

What gets us children of the modern age into trouble is our casual and quite unbiblical tossing around of *love*. In our conversations, it connotes everything and nothing. Because its definition can never be taken for granted, serious writers must pause to define before they employ it. Let me quote just a few definitions at random to show you what I mean:

> Love is the word used to label the sexual excitement of the young, the habituation of the middle-aged, and the mutual dependence of the old.[3]
>
> (John Ciardi)

> Love is the will to extend oneself for the purposes of nurturing one's own or another's spiritual growth.[4]
>
> (Scott Peck)

> It is the energetic and beneficent good will which stops at nothing to secure the good of the beloved object. It isn't primarily an emotion or an affection. It is primarily an active determination of the will.[5]
>
> (C. H. Dodd)

This last definition sent my memory back to my college undergraduate days when my professors offered their definition of biblical love. It is, they said, "intelligent good will." The term is forever fixed in my mind because I was doing some serious dating in those days and wondered how my proposal would sound when on bended knee I would propose to my intended, "I am offering you all my intelligent good will." Somehow I doubted it would sweep her off her feet.

Even though "intelligent good will" may not be the appropriate language to use when you're proposing marriage, it remains a helpful definition. Love *is* intelligent, it is *good*, and it *wills* the best on behalf of somebody else. Love desires the best for the person loved.

If you are serious about wanting to learn love, the best sourcebook for your study is the Bible. Love is its central theme, its reason for being, its passionate message:

> For God so loved the world that he gave his one and only Son, that whoever believes in him shall not perish but have eternal life (John 3:16).

Because of love God gave – sacrificed – his very best. Sacrifice, God wants us to understand, is the essence of love.

Hate is often assumed to be the opposite of love. But consider this: when love moves out, apathy rather than hatred moves in. Hatred is usually love gone sour—bitter but not forgetting, still thinking, still passionately caring. It is intelligent *bad* will, emotionally motivated, cursing whom it once blessed. Apathy no longer cares what happens, for better or worse; haters, on the other hand, are still the emotional prisoners of their former love.

Thus apathy, not hatred, is love's strongest enemy, or so I used to believe until I listened to Harvey Cox on the subject:

> The opposite of love is not hatred; it is possessiveness, the deep-

27

set human drive to control and own the other.[6]

At least we agree in denying hatred the honor. I confess he may have a stronger biblical position than mine, insisting as he does that the scriptures are not naive about this human inclination. Love, it seems, as I try to hold on to a shred of my former conviction, can degenerate into either apathy or possessiveness, into not caring or not caring enough to control. In either case, compassion, or even better, intelligent good will, has fled.

Many marriages disintegrate, for example, when the partners profess love while playing their power games. They act well their charade of marital obligations for propriety's sake, but neither mate is fool enough to think they are playing for love. What began in romance has plummeted to routine. Though they no longer care for one another, they care about their power in the relationship. They have their rights. They possess their places. And they will fight for them.

Perhaps I am too hard on the couple. They were probably duped in the beginning, like most of our society. They confused their infatuation with love. More probably it was lust, which is nearly irresistible, but ever so fickle. It knows little of sacrifice and nothing of loyalty. It's too fragile to endure. Possessiveness and apathy defeat it without contest.

Love, however, is tough; it can sacrifice and it can endure. As far as the Bible is concerned, genuine love is God-centered and God-initiated. He is the source and standard, the authority on and the dynamic in love. God's love is too great for words; language alone can't express it. Real lovers know this, of course, so they act out their love. God knows it best of all, so he dramatized it for us. Only his drama didn't call for an actress; it required a cross.

Like all love, God's was not to be expressed just once. Love

must be acted out again and again. Remembrances of a kindness warms the heart, but in time, memories fade and doubts
crowd in, so God acted out his love as a model to be imitated
rather than a final statement to be recalled. John removes the
action from the stage called Calvary to the one on which we
act:

> This is how we know what love is: Jesus Christ laid down his
> life for us. *And we ought to lay down our lives for our broth-
> ers* (1 John 3:16, 17).

LOVE ACTED OUT:
WE OUGHT TO LAY DOWN
OUR LIVES FOR OUR BROTHERS
1 JOHN 3:16

God didn't put on his passion play for our applause. John
says he had in mind something ongoing. He invites us into the
play; we are to take Christ's role.

When I had come this far in my meditation on love, I stalled.
What more could I say about it? What advice could I offer?
Although I have spent a lifetime learning love, I can speak
Christ's words and act his role clumsily at best. I sat staring at
the screen, fingers hovering over the keyboard, unable to write
any more. Then help came from an unexpected source: my
typing. It is, you might say, creative. I could go so far as to call
it surprisingly suggestive. I am often surprised that the keys I
have mistakenly hit suggest a line of thought had not intended
to take. As I read what I had written above, I came to the quo-
tation, "We ought to lay down our lives for our brothers," but
my independent fingers had something quite different in mind.

They typed, "We ought to lay down our lives for our *bothers*."

Of course. We do that all the time, don't we? Bothered about this, that, or something else, we "lay down our lives," that is, we expend our energies and we deplete our money and other resources to tend the bothers. This is not entirely bad, so long as "our *brothers*" are our most important bothers.

G. K. Chesterton observed that "the Bible tells us to love our neighbors, and also to love our enemies; probably because they are generally the same people."[7] Neighbors, too, can a bother.

Bible-based living isn't easy, as a young seminarian discovered. He was trying his best to make it his guide and standard in all things. He loved God, yearning to serve Him with all his heart, wanting his every action to please the Lord. But he had fallen in love with a beautiful woman and, inexperienced in courting, he felt overwhelmed. He wanted to express his love, to kiss her good night. He'd been dating her for some time, but on every date the ritual was the same. He walked her back to her dormitory, they stood on the steps, he looked deeply and longingly into her eyes, shook her hand – and went home. His problem was that he couldn't locate the scripture he was seeking to justify giving in to his desire to kiss her.

At last he thought he had found it: Romans 16:16, "Greet one another with a holy kiss," though when he checked it out with his professor, he learned the reference had nothing to do with dating. Since he still had no biblical justification for kissing her good night, he continued to restrain himself, and the ritual remained the same. Their evenings together closed with the inevitable but awkward handshake.

One night everything suddenly changed. As usual he walked her back to the dormitory, and as usual they stood on the steps where, as usual, he looked longingly into her eyes and, as usual, shook her hand and turned to leave. That's when she grabbed him by the back of the collar, pulled him to herself, pushed him against the wall and planted a kiss on him that lasted until he came up gasping for air and shouting, "Chapter and verse; chapter and verse."

She was ready for him, and as she prepared to plant another firm kiss, she said, "Do unto others as you would have them do unto you."[8] Any strict Bible scholar could charge her with ripping her verse out of context, but who would be so cruel?

To love with a biblical love is far more demanding than the seminarian's search for a verse giving him permission to act out his feelings. There is no need to mount a search for scriptures on love, since the Bible teems with them. We know what we are supposed to do. We just don't want to do it.

LOVE ACTED OUT FINANCIALLY
1 JOHN 3:17

"If anyone has material possessions and sees his brother in need but has no pity on him, how can the love of God be in him?" (1 John 3:17).

Here's a stiff challenge, one made all the more difficult as our possessions increase. We are surrounded by needy people. But can we love them? And how?

With what we possess, John says. Giving puts love-ability to the test. Everything we own is placed in the service of love. Disciples of Jesus cannot cheat in business deals or take unfair advantage of another; they will go the second mile in helpfulness and will consider their business and financial transactions as opportunities to express the love of God. Money is not an end itself but a means, a conveyor of love. This is why Christians will suffer inequities before they will "take" somebody else.

I'm aware the last paragraph sounds almost foolishly idealistic. It has the ring of ivory-towered thinking, dropped from above by someone who has never had to make a living in what we like to call a "dog eat dog" world. You may be tempted to stop reading and turn for advice to a more realistic adviser.

Don't leave. What I wrote didn't come from the safe confines of my study; it came from the real world. I've had to apply this advice many times. A few years ago, for example, I took the counsel of my financial advisor and invested along with several others in one of those "you can't lose" business deals in which, frankly, all of us lost heavily. My advisor learned a hard lesson about human nature. When the venture collapsed because of the corporation president's dishonesty, some of my friend's partners accused him of willfully leading them into the bad investment, although in each case they had asked him for the opportunity to invest with him in this "sure deal." Some of them had been his friends for years. At the time I didn't know any of this. He lives in another state and I was not aware of the pressure he was under when I wrote to assure him our friendship meant more to me than the money I lost. In time, I was certain, I could recover from the losses through hard work and wiser investing. The money was replaceable; our friendship was not. He wasn't to blame and I didn't hold him liable. Only later did he tell me I was the only one of the investors who offered this reassurance.

Circumstances sometimes force us to choose what we value most of all. More than once I've been disconcerted to discover how many self-proclaimed disciples of Jesus are really Marxists in Christian clothing. They protest their devotion to Jesus, but money determines their behavior. They use people to get things. They boast about the great deals they pulled off with no remorse for causing or profiting from another's losses. What matters isn't the person, but the deal. They don't serve God, but Mammon (Matt 6:24).

If you think I'm exaggerating, let me invite you to listen in on a family fighting over their late father's estate. See them turn against each other, like vultures circling over carrion, anger rising and courtesy evaporating as they quarrel heatedly over their "rightful share." Battle is joined; they will be alienated from one another the rest of their days. Nothing, including their relationships, matters as much as "what I've got coming to me."

When John advises us to lay down our lives for our brothers, he isn't specifically speaking of giving up money, but I have taken us on this little detour to point out the power of possessions, which can drive away even our closest loved ones. When money or what money can buy calls the shots, it is impossible for us to imitate the love of Christ.

LOVE ACTED OUT PERSONALLY
1 JOHN 3:18

Talk of imitating Christ is not enough.

Dear children, let us not love with words or tongue but *with actions and in truth* (1 John 3:18).

I can't ever read these words without hearing Eliza Doolittle in *My Fair Lady*, "Don't talk of love. Show me."

It's time for another typing lesson. While working on a sermon some time ago, I thought I was typing *sweetheart*, but my independent fingers pecked out *sweatheart*, which is an improvement on the original, don't you think? If sweethearts won't be sweathearts, then they won't be sweethearts for long. Work, sacrifice, toil, sweat, and (yes, Churchill was right) tears are the stuff of love. Words are never enough.

LOVE AS THE PROOF OF THE TRUTH
1 JOHN 3:19

Several generations ago, Dr. E. Stanley Jones, whose missionary work in India has been such an inspiration, was traveling in South Africa when he noted a sign in the bathroom of a railroad station: "Please leave this basin in the condition in which you would like to find it." The station manager had borrowed liberally from Jesus: "In everything, do to others what you would have them do to you" (Matt 7:12). Even public bathrooms can be kept clean if the people who use them apply this very simple principle of love. Shortly after visiting the room, reporters asked Dr. Jones whether he had a message for their country and her problems. "Yes," he said, "if you will apply the principle of keeping that bathroom clean, the problems of South Africa will be solved."9 All the words in all the treaties and agreements invoked by the nation's warring factions avail nothing until enough South Africans learn how to keep public bathrooms clean. Have you been hearing James in the background?

What good is it, my brothers, if a man claims to have faith
but has no deeds? Can such faith save him? Suppose a brother

34

or sister is without clothes and daily food. If one of you says to him, Go, I wish you well; keep warm and well fed, but does nothing about his physical needs, what good is it? In the same way, faith by itself, if it is not accompanied by action, is dead. (James 2:14-17).

John would have us prove our *love* by through truth and action; *faith* also must be acted out, James adds. Paul combines these thoughts, making *love* (love-in-action, the only true love) the means by which faith proves itself:

> The only thing that matters is *faith* expressing itself through *love*. (Gal 5:6).

LOVE AS A CLEAR CONSCIENCE, AS CONFIDENCE BEFORE GOD 19-21 1 JOHN 3:19-21

When faith in the Lord expresses itself as active love toward others, then the believer enjoys the peace of a clear conscience before God.

> This then is how we know that we belong to the truth, and how we set our hearts at rest in his presence whenever our hearts condemn us. For God is greater than our hearts, and he knows everything. Dear friends, if our hearts do not condemn us, we have confidence before God . . . .

With nothing to hide, with no lies to cover up, with no malicious motives driving us, we are at ease even in the presence of God.

LOVE AS OBEDIENCE
1 JOHN 3:22-24

In our era, which pontificates about "rights" and has little to say about responsibilities, the scriptural union of *love* and *obedience* is not a popular one. Who likes to be told to "submit to one another," even if it is "out of reverence for Christ"? (Eph 5:21). Submission is obedience and obedience is for children.

During the early days of my marriage, I didn't understand very much about submission. That my wife was to submit to me, her husband, was quite clear to me, though. I didn't know then but I had to learn it in a hurry if our marriage was to survive those first rocky years, that even the head of the house must learn to yield. Then later I had to learn that sometimes parents must submit to their children. When they were right and I was wrong, it profited no one for me to have my own way.

Two things Christians must do, John insists: We must believe in the name of God's Son, Jesus Christ, and we must love one another as he commanded us. Only two things. If we will do them, then we will "live in him" and he will live in us.

Throughout this chapter we've focused on energetic love, a natural fruit of faith in God, a gift of God's Spirit. By faith we who love God are released to love others. I cannot love you as much as I would like without loving Another more. As paradoxical as it sounds, only by first giving my heart to God will I have heart enough for you. Do you know Richard Lovelace's lines?

I could not love thee, dear, so much
loved I not honor more. (A similar paradox.)

The right first love makes the secondary love greater. Similarly, love of God elicits a strong desire to obey his commands, and primary among these commands is that we love one another. Loving him means obeying him. Obeying him means I will love you – actively, energetically, unselfishly.

Before there is obedience, though, there is hearing the word to be obeyed. It's a lesson my father taught me. As far as he was concerned, to hear *is* to obey. When he told me to do something, he always made certain I was listening. When he knew I had heard, he trusted I would obey. Or else. First he would give me my instructions. Then he would add, if there was any doubt in his mind, "Did you hear me?" I knew if I said yes, I would have to do it. Hearing without obedience was not acceptable in our home. Love obeys.

But first it listens. Good listening, of course, results from good loving. We will not hear God perfectly unless we hear him lovingly.

Dr. Scott Peck tells of the time he went to a conference on psychology and religion featuring a prominent authority on the subject. As the man began to speak, Dr. Peck was immediately impressed with his expertise, so he listened intently – for an hour and a half. The room was air conditioned, but by the time the speaker had finished, Peck was sweating, his head throbbing, and the back of his neck aching from the strain. He calls his intense listening an act of love.

During the coffee break, Dr. Peck overheard a woman complain, as she chatted with another woman, "Well, he really didn't tell us anything, did he?" Dr. Peck had been captivated by the truth he was learning, but he had gained so much, he said, because of his own act of love, his listening.[10] Love listens and, having heard the word of the Lord, love obeys.

By now it should be apparent that anything as demanding,

37

as costly, as exhausting in all its forms as love, requires super-human strength to sustain it. Only then can it "bear all things, believe all things, hope all things, endure all things, and never end." Love is, as Paul teaches in 1 Corinthians 12-14, "the most excellent way," transcending all other "spiritual gifts," governing their use, directing them especially in the supreme task of "edifying" the church and all its members.

"Serve one another in love," Paul writes in Galatians 5:13-14. "The entire law is summed up in a single command: Love your neighbor as yourself." To do so, his following argument explains, you must "live by the Spirit" and not "gratify the desires of the sinful nature." Even something as exacting as love is possible when the Holy Spirit is the enabler.

The fruit of the Spirit is *love* . . . .

FOR YOUR FURTHER CONSIDERATION

1. What is love?
2. What's wrong with thinking of love as an emotion?
3. Apart from Jesus, what person in your life has exhibited the greatest love? Describe the person.
4. Which is the opposite of love, hatred or apathy?
5. "Love never ends," the Bible says. Why doesn't it? What gives love its staying power?
6. Why does the author say "many self-proclaimed disciples of Jesus are really Marxists in Christian clothing"? He is playing on a central tenant of Marxism, economic determinism: money calls the shots. Is his indictment fair?
7. What is the relationship between love and obedience? When do we outgrow the need to obey other persons?
8. How does the Holy Spirit help us love?

Endnotes

1. My friend E. Ray Jones learned of this true incident from the executive's boss.

2. Ralph Sockman, *Live for Tomorrow*. New York: The Macmillan Company, 1939, p. 89.

3. Quoted in *The Portable Curmudgeon*, compiled by Jon Winokur. New York and Scarborough, Ontario: NAL Books, New American Library, 1987, p. 180.

4. M. Scott Peck, *The Road Less Traveled*. A Touchstone Book. 1978, p. 81.

5. C.H. Dodd, *Gospel and Law: The Relation of Faith and Ethics in Early Christianity*. New York: Columbia University Press, 1951, p. 42.

6. Harvey Cox, *Turning East*. New York: Simon and Schuster, 1977, p. 85.

7. Quoted in *The Portable Curmudgeon*, compiled by Jon Winokur. New York and Scarborough, Ontario: NAL Books, New American Library, 1987, p. 32.

8. Stolen from Bob Russell, *Making Things Happen*. Cincinnati: Standard Publishing Company, 1987, p. 169.

9. E. Stanley Jones, *Is the Kingdom of God Realism?* New York, Nashville: Abingdon-Cokesbury Press, 1940, p. 81.

10. *The Road Less Traveled*. A Touchstone Book, 1978.

JOY 🐦

Philippians 1:4, 5, 25; 2:2, 29, 30; 4:1, 4
"The fruit of the Spirit is love, *joy* . . . ."

In *Surprised By Joy,* C.S. Lewis writes that when he became a Christian, joy entered his life. A new contentment was his, a sense of well-being that left him satisfied while wanting more of the same. Joy always does this.

Like love, joy is basically an attitude or even, if you please, a lifestyle. Don't confuse it with happiness, which depends on "hap," chance or fortune or luck. Joy doesn't hang on external circumstances but depends on God. Hence it can be found in the grimmest of situations.

Again like love, joy is not an emotion, although it influences

41

feelings. Blaise Pascal writes of currents of ecstasy that swept over him, leaving him able only to exult, "Certainty, joy, certainty, feeling, sight, joy. Joy, joy, tears of Joy."[1] Such exuberance can erupt from the joyful soul. (Who hasn't felt it?) But to reduce joy to a feeling is to diminish it.

Dean Inge comes closer to its essence: "Joy as a moral quality is a Christian invention."[2] His discovery bears pondering, though it surprises at first. Morality governs "shoulds" and "oughts" of behavior, civil or social or sexual. Joy is personal, individual, attitudinal, we think. What we will discover, however, is that unlike happiness, joy is inter-personal; it cannot exist apart from relationship, particularly in one's relationship with the Lord, which in turn colors all other ones. Since joy is rooted in relationships, and since relationships are the domain of morality, Dean Inge is correct: Joy is a moral quality. And since it was best modeled and taught by Christ, it could be called a "Christian invention."

In one other aspect, then, joy resembles love: it is both the result and the cause of moral behavior. By examining a few verses of Paul's joyful Epistle to the Philippians, we'll grasp something of this remarkable quality that inspires martyrs to sing at their death and ordinary persons to smile in the face of disaster.

JOY IN PRAYER

In all my prayers for all of you, I always pray with *joy* because of your partnership in the gospel from the first day until now (Phil 1:4, 5).

A mature Christian's prayers encompass far more than the

"gimmies" – Lord, give me this and Lord, give me that – which yield practically no satisfaction and precious few results.

Instead of begging, joyful prayers give thanks. Mrs. Miller is a good model.[3] Following the removal of her cancerous breast, she lay on a gurney in the hospital hallway. Her daughter says she thinks the nurses left her there on purpose because of her bright, positive spirit. On a gurney beside her lay another lady, sobbing.

"What's the matter, what's wrong?" Mrs. Miller asked.

"What do you mean, what's wrong? Look where I am. I've got cancer."

"So do I."

"Yes, but I had surgery for the removal of one breast and now I've got lumps on the other side."

"So have I."

"But that's not all. These treatments make me violently ill."

"I know, me too."

"Besides all that, I'm in my 50's and I think I'm going to die!"

"I think I am, too."

"Well, how can you lie there so *@+ peaceful?!"

The woman's profanity didn't shock Mrs. Miller. She merely asked, "Have you tried praying?"

"Of course I've prayed! I've gone to every church in our area. I've prayed everything from Christian Scientist to Buddhist and Baptist, and you know what? None of them worked."

"I know why."

"You do? Why?"

"You didn't pray with faith. You have a terrible need in your life. Someone told you to go see the King and petition him to help you. So without preparation or invitation, you barged into the King's throne room. You yelled, 'OK, King, I've got cancer, and You had better do something about it. You gave it to me, king, so You'd better take it back!' Then, because you were so sure he wouldn't help you, you stormed out of his palace without even waiting for a reply. You told your friends and relatives, 'See, I told you so! I went to see the King, and He didn't hear me or help me!'"

Mrs. Miller told her how simple it would have been if she'd gone before the King of all Kings in humility and confessed her sins. How easy it would have been if she had then presented in faith her unbearable need, asking for Him to go through the valley with her, confessing her need for strength and for His help, believing that He would never leave her or forsake her. The lady began sobbing again. Mrs. Miller added, "You think your essential problem is to get rid of cancer, but what you really need is Jesus."

At this point, the lady asked, "Please pray for me now."

Later the nurses reported they had never seen such a dramatic change in a patient. She was never depressed again. In fact, she was like a new woman. She had learned that you can express joy in prayer – not when you're bitter, not when you're angry, not when you're demanding, and certainly not when you're stuck in the gimmies, but when what matters more to you than health or healing is your relationship with your Lord, you can relax into the peace and comfort of his companionship, trusting him to keep you safe, no matter what happens.

In fact, your joy will increase as you pray, like Paul, "for all of you." Your prayers then turn outward, other-directed. Feeling secure yourself, your mind is free to think of and pray for others, either those in need or others like these Philippians, whom Paul considers his partners.

JOY IN PARTNERSHIP

> In all my prayers for all of you, I always pray with joy because of your partnership in the gospel from the first day until now . . . . Convinced of this, I know that I will remain, and I will continue with all of you for your progress and *joy* in the faith, so that through my being with you again your *joy* in Christ Jesus will overflow on account of me (Phil 1:4, 5, 25, 26).

Paul's love and appreciation for his friends shines through his use of *partnership*, doesn't it? He has been confident of their standing with him from the beginning of his ministry among them and he expects God to effect a reunion with them when (and if – see verses 21-24) he is released from prison. His thoughts are on them. He desires to be reunited so he can be of help and comfort to them. They are his partners. Notice in these sentences the outwardness of joy. It doesn't focus on itself but on others, and it delights in what it sees.

Here the difference between happiness and joy is obvious. Happiness depends upon the things that touch our lives; joy takes pleasure in the persons who touch us. If the environment is hostile or conditions aren't satisfactory, we become unhappy, but we don't lose our joy.

Not so long ago I was intrigued to read what Gontran de Poncins has written about Eskimos. I suppose I'm fascinated by these hardy people because they are like Arizona's desert dwellers in the pre-air conditioning era. Once I couldn't imagine anyone choosing to live in the desert; now that I live here, I can't imagine anyone dwelling where it's so cold and white and barren. In either case, the temperature extremes are formidable. Yet de Poncins writes,

> Here was a people living in the most rigorous climate of the

world, in the most depressing surroundings imaginable, haunted by famine in a grey and somber landscape sullen with the absence of light; shivering in their tents in the autumn, fighting the recurrent blizzards in the winter, toiling and moiling fifteen hours a day merely in order to get food and stay alive.

It's enough to drive you mad, isn't it? Just reading this paragraph made me realize how dependent on our environment we allow ourselves to become. We need so many things, it seems. Yet it is not so among the Eskimos:

> Huddling and motionless in their igloos through this interminable night, they ought to have been melancholy men, men despondent and suicidal; instead, they were a cheerful people, always laughing, never wearying of laughter.[4]

They don't seem to know they're supposed to be unhappy. They don't have the newest cars; they're deprived of television sets and computers and the myriad other electronic geegaws the rest of us demand. They are bereft of the sun for weeks on end. Yet they are neither despondent nor suicidal. How do you account for such people? They are proof of joy's independence of things or circumstances and its dependence on people. Joy may be found wherever persons take pleasure in fellowship, which is partnership by another name. What the Eskimos de Poncins observes have learned often eludes us. The truth is that you cannot buy enough things or control your environment carefully enough to manufacture joy. The product of good fellowship, it inheres in relationships, not possessions.

A journalist once asked Bill Blass, the famous clothing designer, whether he minded traveling and talking to so many people. Blass confessed, "Actually, I find it interesting. But you do get tired of smiling."[5] Is it possible? How can a person get tired of smiling? Yes, your facial muscles may ache with the strain of prolonged beaming, but while your face grows weary *from* smiling, it's certainly not tired *of* smiling, is it? Perhaps so, especially if, like J. Alfred Prufrock in T. S. Eliot's famous love poem, you have *prepared* "a face to meet the faces that you meet." When a smile is only skin deep, keeping it going grows tiresome, I suppose. If you have to freeze a smile on your face to deal with people you don't like or to pull off a deal that isn't right, smiling does grow tedious.

On the other hand, haven't you been with friends who've had you laughing so hard your face and sides hurt? Your muscles ache from the laughter – but you aren't tired *of* laughing or smiling. When laughter comes from the inside out, as an overflow of joy, you don't get tired of it.

We're not at all like U. S. newspaper editor Emile Henry Gauvreau, who described himself as being "part of that strange race of people aptly described as spending their lives doing things they detest to make money they don't want to buy things they don't need to impress people they dislike."[6] There's a life for you! No joy for him.

We turn back to Paul, who has found joy in abundance.

JOY IN LOVE AND UNITY

> If you have any encouragement from being united with Christ, if any comfort from his love, if any fellowship with the Spirit, if any tenderness and compassion, then make my joy complete by being like-minded, having the same love, being one in spirit and purpose (Phil 2:1, 2).

Paul's request for his friends to "make my joy complete" expresses a very human longing. Nothing pleases us more than knowing the people we love love the other people we love. What greater reward can parents experience than watching their children treating each other with love?

One of Charles Schultz' classic Peanuts cartoons depicts Linus placidly watching his favorite television program. His reverie is rudely interrupted when Lucy comes in. Immediately she starts grumbling because she wants to watch *her* favorite. Linus tries to defend himself. "Give me one good reason," he tells her, "why I should turn from my program to yours."

The ever-blunt Lucy says has her answer ready. "See my hand? Individually and alone each finger is quite weak, but joined together they make a fist!"

He says, "Okay, okay, I get the point. What program was it you wanted?" As he walks away, he's looking at his hand and plaintively asking, "Why can't you guys ever get together like that?"[7]

What the apostle Paul wants is for "guys" like you and me to get together like that (although not in order to threaten a brother), united in mind, in love, in spirit, and in purpose. In such love and unity is joy to be found.

JOY IN GIVING HONOR

People who love one another get their greatest "kicks" from honoring each other. In 2:29, 30 Paul refers to his good friend Epaphroditus. The Philippian church had dispatched him to minister on their behalf to the imprisoned Paul. While with him Epaphroditus became so dangerously ill his friends feared for his life. Now recovered, he is ready to return home with Paul's blessing:

Welcome him in the Lord with great joy, and honor men like

him, because he almost died for the work of Christ, risking his life to make up for the help you could not give me (Phil 2:29, 30).

"Welcome and honor him in the Lord. He has deserved your praise." Unless specifically looking for the connection, we could read this passage without seeing the relationship among "welcome," "honor," and "joy."

I might have missed the connection myself, if I had not had the privilege on several occasions to pay tribute to someone. One of my most cherished memories, for example, is of a memorial service. When Aldis Webb's family asked me to officiate at his funeral service, I must have startled them with the eagerness of my response. Nothing but an extreme emergency could have kept me away. Dr. Webb was my pastor, my mentor – my Paul. While I am indebted to many others for their influence on my life (people like Dr. Jess Johnson, who later did so much go guide my development in ministry, and Vivian Mondhan, who has been friend, confidante, and counselor since my youth), Aldis Webb was my minister during most of the formative years of my youth. He baptized me and later ordained me into the ministry. His preaching, example, and private advice molded much of my thinking. I owed – and owe – him beyond repayment.

How can I tell you the extent of my joy in telling everyone at that service just how much I loved and respected this man?

Praise invites and expresses joy; criticism, on the other hand, drives it away.

The pleasure of receiving honor melts to nothingness when compared with the joy of honoring. On a few occasions I have been the glad recipient of this or that award or presentation, and I confess to relishing such moments. Never, however, have

I received any honor that has compared with the sheer over-flowing elation experienced when I have been able to pay tribute to someone else.

I experience that pleasure at least once a year. The elders in our church host an annual "Elder-Staff Appreciation Banquet." The highlight of the evening is the presentation of plaques to the minister and the support staff-member of the year. As the senior minister, I get to "do the honors." It's my chance to say publicly what I've thought of the honorees privately.

You have done the same thing, haven't you? Why do you go to so much trouble to throw a birthday party for somebody? Certainly it isn't to celebrate age. No, the birthday is merely an excuse to pay homage to someone you love. (Oh yes, I know that in some offices these parties are mandatory. I'm not talking about the ones you have to put on, but those you want to.)

Students of American society have for some time now been bewailing the loss of simple etiquette. The decline should not surprise us, should it? You can't have it both ways. You can't tout the primacy of individual rights on the one hand and then expect to see a flourishing of courtesy on the other. It only stands to reason that if I love me (as my society has taught me to) and I put myself first (simply a matter of looking out for Number One), then you'll just have to wait your turn for my attention. You'll never be better than first after me.

Me-firsters never perceive the joy of honoring; they are ignorant of the pleasure taken in the old-fashioned chivalry of a person like Robert E. Lee. Just one little incident depicts his character. He was riding in the coach of a train nearly filled with his soldiers when a lady boarded the train and entered their coach. Starting at one end she walked the entire length of the aisle between the seats until she approached General Lee's seat.

50

When he spotted her, the general stood to give her his seat. His soldiers, observing their commander's courtesy, stood to a man, each offering to give him his seat. He would not take one, explaining he could not accept from them an honor they had denied a lady.

Honoring other persons eventually becomes habitual, the natural corollary of love. Paul makes this relationship explicit elsewhere (Rom 12:9-11):

> Love must be sincere. Hate what is evil; cling to what is good. Be devoted to one another in brotherly love. *Honor one another above yourselves.*

Are you having trouble getting along with someone at home or work? Do you find another person constantly irritating you? Have you ever questioned the source of the tension? Is it possible you have been dwelling on how you ought to be treated instead of seeking ways to honor, even if only in small acts of courtesy, the one who's on your nerves? Try to "honor another above yourself;" you very well could be surprised by joy, which always rewards the giver, but withholds itself from the withholder of honor.

JOY IN FRIENDSHIP

Joy is one of the supreme rewards of friendship. Listen to Paul's exuberant language:

> Therefore, my brothers, you whom I love and long for, my *joy* and crown, that is how you should stand firm in the Lord, dear friends! (Phil 4:1).

These beloved Philippians are his brothers, his longed-for-ones, his joy, his dear friends, his crown (the prize of ultimate achievement).

What joy there is in friendship. I was glad the members of my congregation couldn't see my behavior a couple years ago when friend Allan Dunbar and I conducted a city-wide crusade in the civic auditorium in Charlottestown. Allan ministers in Calgary, Alberta now, but when he was younger he lived in Charlottestown, so for him the week was a sentimental reunion with his old territory and friends. We have had a good time in each other's company for a long time, even though he's 6'4" tall and I'm not. Through some careless planning on the part of the nominating committee, the year I was president of the North American Christian Convention, he was named vice president. One of his most memorable comments that year – out of the host of irreverencies he uttered – was the one spoken before the one hundred twenty members of the planning committee: "We make a great team, Roy. I can just put you up on my knee and work you from behind (like a dummy)."

Well, we liberally sprinkled that same pathetic humor over our program in P.E.I. About midweek the host minister called us into his office and gently but firmly reprimanded us for misbehaving in public and possibly bringing shame to the Lord. We took our chastisement like well-mannered schoolboys and then that night (I say this with a blush) carried on as usual. We weren't showing off. We weren't even trying to be funny. We were merely celebrating our friendship in the Lord. I'm afraid we misbehave whenever we're together; such is the delight we take in each other's company.

Our experience in Canada caused me to reflect again on the wise words of George MacDonald: "It is the heart that is not yet sure of its God that is afraid to laugh in His presence."[8]

A heart that is not yet sure of a friend cannot laugh in his presence, either. A family whose members are unsure of one another dwell in a house without laughter. A marriage teetering on the precipice finds little to laugh about.

Where there is real friendship, however, where there is mutual understanding and acceptance and tolerance and pleasure in one another's company, there is joy. I'm belaboring the obvious; you already know this. Your face lights up when you see a good friend approaching. No sight is more pleasant, is it?

Joy, as all of the above has testified, is relational. Jesus pays such a relationship the supreme compliment as he talks to his closest friends:

> I have told you all these things so that my joy may be in you and that your joy may be complete. My commandment is this: Love each other as I have loved you (John 15:11, 12).

Do you recall what I said in the beginning of this book? The Spirit works for the unity of everything in him, so the fruit of the Spirit is an aggregate of inseparables. The fruit is singular, composed of love, joy, peace, patience, and so on. In speaking with his disciples here, Jesus brings joy and love together. My *joy* is in you if you *love* one another. Your *love* makes me *joyful*.

> Greater love has no one than this, that one lay down his life for his friends. You are my friends if you do what I command. I no longer call you servants, because a servant does not know his master's business. Instead, I have called you friends, for everything that I learned from my Father I have made known to you (John 15:13-15).

This is the direction the Christian life takes. We begin by trusting and obeying the Lord. What begins as submission, though, ends in a friendship so close we know our Friend's mind and he knows ours. The lowly student has become an honored friend.

I had an experience like this with one of my major professors. I revered the man's brilliance; he was kind and in all things good. One day, as we went for a walk together, I realized Professor Mc Donough was treating me as almost an equal, certainly as a trusted friend. The disciple (student) was being honored as a friend. How I savored the conversations, sought his advice, and delighted in his presence.

That is the metamorphosis we experience in our walk with Christ. Starting out timidly, conscientiously trying to follow him, we discover somewhere along the way – it happens before we're aware of it – that his arm is around us and ours around him. He has accepted us a friends, and we respond with joy.

JOY IN THE LORD ALWAYS

Paul's final word on the subject is, surprisingly, a command:

Rejoice in the Lord always. I will say it again: Rejoice! (Phil 4:4).

Rejoice is in the imperative mood, an order. The grammar implies that we have control over whether or not we will obey it. Rejoicing, then, is not something that happens to us (like happiness). Rejoicing is something have the power to do or not to do. The choice is ours.

How can we rejoice in the Lord? First, we must *decide* to be in the Lord. To be "in the Lord" is quite similar to being "in business." It's what we do, who we are. If affects how we walk, talk, think, dress, associate. For a businessman, being "in business" is inseparable from his character, his personality, his essence.

If that analogy seems inadequate, let me try another. Being "in the Lord" is like being "in love." The first time you ever confessed to being "in love," what did you mean? Wasn't it that that everything about you – your thinking, feelings, willing, dressing, playing, dreaming – everything was altered by this new preoccupation? You thought you would never be the same again. (And if you stayed in love, you weren't.) Being in love is a state of being.

Being in Christ is also. And a dominant characteristic of this "in Christ" state is *joy*.

Thomas Chalmers claimed there are three grand essentials of happiness. By "happiness" he meant what I mean by joy:

Something to do,
Something to love,
Something to hope for.[9]

Christ gives us all three:

We *do* the commission he has given his disciples
We *love* him and *love* those he loves
We *hope* for life abundant and eternal

Thus we find joy.

FOR YOUR FURTHER CONSIDERATION

1. What do you think the author means, "Joy is a lifestyle"?

2. How would you differentiate between happiness and joy?

3. How important are other people to a joyful person?

4. What kinds of things make you unhappy? What can rob you of your joy?

5. In Philippians 2:29, 30 Paul writes of his friend Epaphroditus. In the passage the words "welcome," "honor," and

"joy" appear to be closely related. How?

6. Which would you rather do, receive an honor or bestow one? Why?

7. Why are manners important to joy?

8. Describe your best friendship. What part does joy play in it?

9. Can you think of something even better than joy? What is it?

Endnotes

1. Quoted in Rufus M. Jones, *The Testimony of the Soul.* New York: The Macmillan Company, 1936, p. 21.

2. Quoted in E. Stanley Jones, *Christ and Human Suffering.* Nashville: Abingdon Press, 1933, p. 121.

3. Mrs. Miller is the mother of Joyce Landorf, who tells this story in *The Fragrance of Beauty.* Wheaton, IL, Victor Books, 1973, pp. 38-41.

4. Quoted in Harry Emerson Fosdick, *On Being a Real Person.* New York & London: Harper & Brothers, 1943, p. 201.

5. "A Bill Blass Sampler," *TWA Ambassador,* September 1983, p. 60.

6. Quoted in Jerry White, *Honesty, Morality and Conscience.* Colorado Springs: Navpress, 1979, pp. 61, 62.

7. Quoted from John Wade, "Peanuts and Unity," *The Lookout,* October 25, 1981, p. 12.

8. *George MacDonald, an Anthology,* ed. C. S. Lewis. Fount paperbacks, 1946, p. 132.

9. Quoted in *Leadership* Magazine, Fall 1988, p. 93.

PEACE ❧

JOHN 14:27

"The fruit of the Spirit is love, joy, *peace* . . . ."

CHRIST'S PEACE IS CONDITIONAL

Peace I leave with you; my peace I give you. I do not give to
you as the world gives. Do not let your hearts be troubled and
do not be afraid (John 14:27).

It isn't for everybody, this Christ-promised, Holy Spirit-deliv-
ered peace; it's special and conditional.

I remember how surprised I was when I first read the words
of the angels to the shepherds in something other than the

King James Version. Like every other Sunday School child, I had memorized the "correct" speech: "Glory to God in the highest and on earth peace, good will toward men." It's always a little dismaying to learn that what one has known forever isn't right. The *New International Version* offers a better translation of the angels' proclamation: "Glory to God in the highest, and on earth peace to men on whom His favor rests." Peace is not promised to everyone, and it is not available merely for the asking.

In another well-known passage, the Apostle Paul writes,

And the peace of God which transcends all understanding will guard your heart and your mind in Christ Jesus (Phil 4:5).

Once again, the proffered peace isn't for everybody, but for those "in Christ Jesus." Earlier Paul had written,

Rejoice in the Lord always. I will say it again: Rejoice! Let your gentleness be evident to all (Phil 4:4).

"In the Lord" here is identical to "in Christ Jesus" in the former passage. This peace is possible if you are "in Him" and if you will not be

. . . anxious about anything, but in everything, by prayer and petition, with thanksgiving, present your requests to God (Phil 4:6).

This peace "transcends all understanding." You can't really explain it. You definitely can't reduce it to a mere absence of stress, which is how we popularly define it. Jesus, in fact, promises just the opposite.

Do not think that I came to bring peace on earth. No, I tell you, I came to bring division (Luke 12:51).

His words sound uncharacteristically harsh until we remember how frequently he alludes to the spiritual warfare disturbing this planet and splitting humanity into hostile camps. The forces of Christ deceive themselves if they think they'll be admired by the enemy's troops.

There is definitely no absence of stress on a battlefield, or on the home front, either. Analyze the daily calendars of the people in your circle; you'll quickly find many who are suffering stress overload. Aren't you sometimes tempted to shout (as I do in my unoriginal way), "Stop the world, I want to get off"? If you'd ask me about my frustrations, I'd insist that all I want is a little peace and quiet. Just let me alone, don't talk to me, don't ask me anything, don't ask anything of me. Just give me absolute, complete, total absence of stress, and hurry!

Absence of stress. That's definitely not the peace that Jesus promises. He knows what we admit in our honest moments: it's not possible, not even healthful, to live without stress. Physicians now tell us that pressure in itself isn't harmful. It's the kind of tension that matters, and how it's handled. It is possible, even in a high-pressured existence, to experience peace. You won't though, if that's your primary objective. Peace does not come first. Even in Galatians 5:22, the basis for this study, peace takes third place. First comes the love for God and others, followed by love's natural consequence and companion, joy. Give love and joy priority in your life, and personal peace is inevitable. Reverse the order, and the peace you seek so desperately will stay just out of reach.

What distraught father hasn't groaned, "If I could just get a little peace in this house." You can count on it – he'll never get it, not so long as it's what he wants most from his family. "When I come home from a hard day's work, all I want is to be left alone." An understandable desire, to be sure, but elusive. It's too self-centered. Jesus did not promise, "Blessed are those who yearn for peace," but "Blessed are those who *make* peace." The necessary ingredients for making peace are, in the first place, as we've already noted, love and joy. The recipe also calls for patience, kindness, gentleness, faithfulness, and self-control. Peace requires, sorry to say, hard work. We recognize this on the international scene; it's always much easier to wage war than to preserve peace.

So far I've been writing as if attaining harmony were a strictly human endeavor. There's more, though. If peace is what you really want, you must begin the process of attaining it by putting things back together between you and God. The biblical word is *reconciliation*. You must start here because your renewed friendship with God will lead immediately to a rekindled sensitivity to other people and a desire to repair the relationships you've damaged.

The Old Testament very often couples peace and righteousness, and the New Testament book of Hebrews designates Christ both King of Righteousness and King of Peace. Right living, or righteousness, is fundamental to peace.

So I repeat: Christ's peace is conditional; it is not for everybody, and never merely for the asking. Nor is it to be equated with the absence of stress, nor given top priority. Right relationships are.

Perhaps the best picture of this hard-won quality comes from the early days of human aviation. Seeking to understand and thus predict how hurricanes behave, meteorologists flew aboard an Army Air Corps plane directly into a furious storm. Their findings are old stuff now, but what they learned on that flight astonished them. They penetrated the hurricane's center fear-ing its fury, but instead they flew into an eerie peace. One of men later asserted he would never again be afraid of a hurricane if he could just get to its eye. Since that pioneering flight, "the eye in the hurricane" has become a cliche describing peace of mind in the midst of harassment.

CHRIST'S PEACE IS BESTOWED

This peace we are talking about is bestowed, not wrested. Jesus says it very simply: "Peace I *leave* with you; my peace I *give* you." It doesn't yield to striving; it seldom responds to our ritual or ceremony or prescribed exercises. It is, as Jesus says, a gift.

Paul writes of it more at length in Romans.

> Therefore since we have been justified through faith, we have peace with God through our Lord Jesus Christ (Rom 5:1).

That word *justified* comes directly from the courtroom. You are standing before the judge. You have been accused, tried, and found guilty. But another assumes your guilt and pays the penalty you owe. The judge declares you innocent and releases you. You aren't innocent, but you receive the deference due the blameless. Until now you've been distracted by guilt, dreading possible exposure, worried about what would happen when you were found out.

Now you've been discovered and your guilt exposed, but it doesn't matter. You won't be punished. Gratitude replaces your fear. You leave the courtroom in genuine, unpursued freedom.

The highest court has set you free and you cannot be tried again on these charges.

All that was required of you was your belief in the Justifier.

The account of a nearly fatal speedboat accident helps us approach the subject from another perspective. The driver was pushing his craft through the water at its top speed when suddenly he veered into a wave at the wrong angle. In an instant the boat flipped crazily and catapulted him so deep into the lake that for a moment he didn't know which way was up. If you've never had this experience you might not be aware how frightening it is. You can't tell where the surface is. Afraid you'll not make it before your lungs burst, you flail about, wasting precious energy and moments in pure panic. Fortunately this man wasn't a novice; he knew what he had to do, which was nothing. He forced himself to remain calm and wait. Soon the buoyancy of his life vest lifted him upward. Sensing the direction, he stroked through the water and burst through the surface just before his air gave out.

Capsized boaters are not alone in wondering which way is up. How hard we try to make the right decisions, to do the right things, to go to the right places, to be seen with the right people, hoping but not quite certain we are moving upward or will get there in time. We borrow for our own times President Lincoln's assessment of the Civil War's darkest days: "The occasion is piled high with difficulty and we must rise high with the occasion." But how do we rise?

With spiritual help.

And it's available. "The Spirit helps us in our weakness." Therefore, "we are more than conquerors" (Rom 8:26, 37).

The Christian's peace of mind comes from the consciousness that the Spirit of God is always with him, no matter where he is. There is comfort in another's presence, a fact Joy frequently reminds me about. She and I often find ourselves in

62

hotels in large city neighborhoods where it's not safe to go out alone. Joy flatters me by wanting me to accompany her, saying she feels safer when I'm a long. She says she's not afraid when she can take my hand. With me she feels safe. She's not being totally rational, of course. What kind of help does she think I could be if we were accosted? I won't carry a gun, I don't know karate, and I'm littler than 90 per cent of any would-be assailants. She seems to have no real appreciation of her situation when she says my presence gives her peace. Nor does she know how much braver I feel because she's with me!

Even when we're not together, though, neither of us is alone. Having received assurance of God's presence with us through his Spirit, we "did not receive a spirit that makes (us slaves) again to fear, but (we) received the Spirit of sonship" (Rom 8:15). As children of the living God, we have no reason to be afraid.

With piqued curiosity I picked up a book entitled *Zen and the Art of Motorcycle Maintenance* by Robert Pirsig. (Who could resist such a title, especially a motorcycle afficionado like me?) It's not really about how to keep a Harley on the road, at least not primarily. It's a book of philosophy, and not even a philosophy I agree with. One paragraph, though, riveted my attention. Pirsig's subject is inner peace which, he says, occurs on three levels of understanding. The first is physical quietness, bringing one's body under discipline so that it can be at peace. This is the easiest level to achieve. The second is mental quietness, in which one has no wandering thoughts. I don't know about you, but that's tough for me to achieve. The third level, however, is the most demanding of all. He calls it value quietness, a stillness in which one has no wandering desires at all.

I wish I could tell you I'm there. The sad truth is I am usually harried by wandering desires. Covetousness is the mark of the beast in almost all of us, isn't it? What a wonderful relief we experience when we can finally say of most things, "Well, I don't really need and don't even want that."

In some areas of my life I can boast that my desires have retired from wandering. Clothes, for example. In my youth I was as fashion-conscious as any normal teenager. That phase didn't last long. Collegiate poverty cured me pretty quickly. Too quickly and too thoroughly, my children believe. When they were still living at home and happened to be out of bed when I left for work, which fortunately didn't happen very often, inevitably one of them would stop me. "Dressed yourself this morning, didn't you, Dad?" To save any further hassles, I would obediently return to the bedroom to start over again.

Memories of that ritual came to mind recently when I had to face up the need for some new shoes. Holes had been worn through my old favorites again. They had been re-soled four times already and they didn't look as if they could survive any further surgery. Consequently I braced myself for battle. I hate shopping. For many years when facing the need for shoes, I've known exactly where to go. A discount shoe store on Southern Avenue never failed me. On the day of this adventure, however, the store was missing. It had moved without leaving a forwarding address. Consternation. I didn't know what to do; for a decade this shop had covered my feet. In my distress, I drove straight home. My comfortable old friends could provide several more months of service, unless it rained, and Arizona receives only about six inches of rain a year. My solution worked – until the first downpour.

I'm not anxious about cars, either. I can contentedly drive anything on wheels.

64

Or houses. I can sleep anywhere.

Personal computers, though, are another matter. My electronic notebook is always with me, whether in a village in India or on the beaches of Hawaii. It's my "brains," and I can hardly function without it. When I dropped my first one on a concrete floor in Bolivia, I was disconsolate until a brilliant Wycliffe Bible Translators technician repaired it in the jungles of Peru. When the floppy disk drive of my top-of-the-line, second one (a Compac LTE 286) quit working, we sent it back to the distributor from whom we had purchased it. This company declared bankruptcy, carrying the Compac into oblivion with it. My loss was like the loss of a reliable friend. My third computer is better than either of the first two. I'm guarding it against all possible danger.

It's easy for me to lose my peace of mind over computers. The peril is in the progress. I read computer magazines, which I shouldn't do, because they just increase my anxiety. New software comes out monthly; new hardware almost as often. No matter how hard I try, I can't keep up with either. When other computer junkies boast of their latest purchases, they depress me. They have something newer or more powerful or faster or equipped with better bells and whistles. Even Mike, our church's executive minister, gives me trouble. Altogether too often, when I am bragging a little about this or that program I'm using, he'll throw in, "You know, I was reading in a magazine about a new program that is much better than that one." With one sentence he renders my stuff obsolete and wipes out my peace of mind.

Why this confession? To encourage yours. Are you, too, guilty of covetousness? Is some niggling little desire stealing your peace of mind?

There's no sin in desiring, of course. It's when the yearnings take control, writing their own agenda, traveling their own route, that sin intrudes and peace is banished. When the the neighbors bring home the very thing we've been wanting, we don't rest until we catch up with – or, even better, surpass them. Their prosperity makes us feel incomplete, dated. Like deprived addicts we yearn for what is out of reach. We can't control desires. We are addicted to our cravings and we can't be helped until we confess, "I need power beyond my own to overcome this problem."

When we reach this stage, we are ready to receive the peace Jesus is ready to bestow.

CHRIST'S PEACE IS UNIQUE

> I have told you these things, so that in me you may have peace. In this world you will have trouble. But take heart! I have overcome the world (John 16:33).

It's a personal peace. "Your peace is in *me*." Paul amplifies on the words of Jesus in Ephesians 2:14:

> For he himself [Jesus] is our peace, who has made the two [the antagonistic Jew and Gentile] one . . . .

In him, because of our separate love for him, old enmities are dissolved. The more "into" Christ you and I are, the less off-putting our dissimilarities become. At peace with him and within ourselves because of our relationship with him, we enjoy increasing harmony with one another.

Paul writes in a similar vein in Colossians 3:15:

> Let the peace of Christ rule in your hearts, since as members of one body you were called to peace.

Once again you'll note that our peace centers in a Person.

66

Secure with him, we see our anxieties and injurious stresses vanish.

Let's return to the weather for a moment, this time to a ship's stormy crossing from Europe to the United States. Giant waves toss the liner about, fraying the passengers' nerves. Unable to sleep, they gather in the lounge, weeping and praying and trying to one another. Then the captain enters. He stands at the doorway for a moment, strong and confident, then smiles as he steps into their company. He quietly tells them of other storms he and his ship have already survived. The engines are doing their job, he assures them. There is no evidence of strain on the ship. "We will trust in our good ship and in God, and He'll bring us through."[1]

The passengers relax. In *him* is peace.

First Thessalonians 5:23 calls our Lord the God of Peace. Centering our lives on him, we are at ease. We know this is so; unfortunately, worrying comes easier than waiting on the Lord. Do you read the newspapers? Every day 5,000 Boeing planes carry passengers safely to their destinations. Did you know that? Probably not. What you know is that every now and then an airplane malfunctions or crashes. For example, on February 24, 1989, a plane lost its cargo door and nine passengers were sucked through the hole. The story was carried on front pages all around the world. Surely the more remarkable story is of the daily safe take-offs and landings of 5,000 commercial passenger planes. Why do you suppose it never makes the front page?

You know the answer. We prefer our news to be bad. We enjoy working ourselves into a frenzy. What then are we to do with the Lord's promise, which says, "I'm giving you my peace"? We are to trust him. We will cast our cares on him. We

67

will teach ourselves to be as observant of the five thousand safe daily flights as we are of the occasional mishap. We will remember and claim the Psalmist's outlook:

Even though I walk
through the valley of the shadow of death,
I will fear no evil,
for you are with me . . . .(Ps 23:4).

When our friends Bobbie and Hubert Ramey attended the funeral of Hubert's long-time Army buddy, Bobbie was so impressed she had to share her reflections with us. Another of Hubert's buddies conducted the service. A deeply committed Christian though not a minister, his words were simple and comforting. When he read the familiar Twenty-third Psalm, he paused to comment, "Just as the shadow of a barking dog cannot bite me, or the shadow of the sharpest sword cannot cut me, so the shadow of death cannot hurt me." He had found the source of peace.

Chuck Swindoll tells this story of his sister Lucy who was driving her car in the Southwest one evening and became aware that a car had been following her for some time. She decided to look for a motel and drove into a small town. The following car made every turn she made, and she became increasingly nervous as she entered the motel to register. She spotted the other car as she came out of the lobby, and quickly drove to her room, entered, and locked the door. While she was taking a shower, she noticed a tipped-up slat in the venetian blind, and imagined whoever was following her was peeking in at her. She was pretty close to panic at this stage, when she noticed a piece of paper under the glass on the dresser top. It said,

Come to me, all who are weary and heavy laden, and I will give you rest. Take my yoke upon you and learn from me, for I am gentle and humble in heart and you shall find rest for your souls (Matt 11:28-29).

An enormous sense of relief filled her. She straightened the slat in the venetian blind, turned out the light and went to bed, where she slept peacefully all night. She had changed the focus of her attention from what was causing her fear to the One who would give her peace.[2]

Henry Drummond, in one of his famous stories, has illustrated true peace. There once was a contest between two artists who were asked to paint something that would portray the idea of rest. The first painter pictured a still, lone lake nestled among forested mountains. It certainly did look restful. The second painter took an entirely different tack. His was a picture of a thundering waterfall cascading off a mountain ridge. At the top of the waterfall, a birch tree bent over the water's foam-flecked surface. In a branch on the birch tree, a robin sat on its nest.

Drummond said the painting of the still lake in the mountains was not a picture of rest but of stagnation. The one of the robin in her nest represented true rest, because it accurately displayed the opposing elements in rest – tranquility and energy, silence and turbulence, creation and destruction, fearlessness and fearfulness. It's easy for us to agree with Drummond, because for Christians, anyway, no matter how precarious our perch, we are not out there alone. Our companion is the Spirit whom Jesus promised us. Whether in a storm at sea or amid the thundering storms of the heart, we can sing "It is well, it is well with my soul."

Shortly before he died in his nineties, I received a treasured letter from Dr. Donald McGavran, one of the outstanding missionary leaders of the twentieth century. I had written to offer condolences on the death of his life-long companion, Mary.

She'd been ill for several years. In the letter, one sent in response to the condolences of his many friends, he talked matter-of-factly about her death. His last three paragraphs perfectly summarize this chapter.

> It is entirely proper and to be expected that the end of my own life, which now seems certain in the next few weeks or months because of colon cancer, should come so soon after her homegoing. I am sure that Mary would join me in hoping that all of you who receive this letter will play an active part in world evangelization. Carrying out the great command of Him to whom all authority in heaven and on earth has been given is something which all Christians ought to be doing.
>
> I trust that God will greatly bless you and extend your life so that your closing years will be full of good works and much effective evangelism. The task yet before us is very large. I pray that God will give to each one of you both insight and strength so that you can carry it out effectively. With much love to you and expecting to meet you beyond the golden gates sometime in the next 50 years, I am,
>
> As ever your comrade in Christ,
> Donald McG

The old missionary is dying as he lived, urging his friends to "get on with the task of evangelism." That, I submit to you, is peace. He is not distressed about the ravages of his disease; he is not fussing over the frailties of age. What I haven't told you is that he was nearly blind when he wrote those words, quite feeble – but in body only. Don McGavran didn't reach the pinnacle of his missionary career until he was retirement age. But then he revolutionized the Christian missionary enterprise in this century. All of us who knew him marveled at his energy.

His was the energy that peace releases. Peace is anything but stagnation. It is controlled, disciplined, joyful energy – the poised power that enables a robin to rest on a thin branch over a raging waterfall, or a single woman to sleep in spite of her earlier fear she was being pursued, or a dying missionary to forget his pain in his plea for others to take up his work after him.

It was, after all, a missionary to earth who said,

My peace I leave with you; my peace I give you.

FOR YOUR FURTHER CONSIDERATION

1. This chapter says peace is conditional. What does it depend on?

2. What's the difference between "absence of stress" and the peace Jesus offers?

3. What is required of a person in order to become a peacemaker?

4. This chapter presents several illustrations in its attempt to find an adequate picture of peace. Of the following, which comes closest: flying in the eye of the hurricane, relaxing into the natural buoyancy of deep waters, walking through potentially dangerous streets with a trusted companion, lying tranquil like a lake in the mountains, or resting on the branch above the roaring waterfall? Do you have a better picture?

5. What is the source of a Christian's peace of mind?

6. What is the "value quietness" Pirsig speaks of? Do you possess it?

7. In your own words, describe the peace that Christ gives us, the peace Paul says we were called to.

8. Think again of Dr. Donald McGavran's state of mind as he faced his impending death. Could you so peacefully prepare to die? What is the secret of his readiness?

Endnotes

1. Dr. Stanley Durkee tells this story, which is quoted in J. Wallace Hamilton, *Ride the Wild Horses.* Westwood, New Jersey, *et al.*: Fleming H. Revell Company, 1952, p. 110.
2. Charles R. Swindoll, *Growing Deep in the Christian Life.* Portland: Multnomah Press, 1986, p. 111.

PATIENCE ❧

Hebrews 6:1-12

"The fruit of the Spirit is love, joy, peace, *patience* . . . ."

This chapter is for me. You are welcome to read it, but you probably don't need it as much as I do. Developing patience has without doubt been my most enduring, most frustrating spiritual battle.

For the fruit of the Spirit is . . . patience.

I believe it. In my case, only the Holy Spirit can effect patience. I haven't been able to develop the virtue on my own, and it isn't that I haven't tried.

Hebrews 6:12 has long been a problematic verse for this

impulsive, impatient disciple:

> We do not want you to become lazy, but to imitate those
> who through faith and patience inherit what has been promised
> (6-12).

What a surprising combination: faith and patience coupled,
laziness opposed to both of them. When you have my temperament, you naturally team patience with laziness and contrast
faith to each. Faith gets things done. Faith is in a hurry, eager
to reach the objective, impatient with obstacles. What laid back
people like to call patience, a Type A achiever scorns as laziness under another name, reasoning that phlegmatic persons
can't work up enough energy to be impatient so they sanctify
their sloth with such time-honored cliches as, "I'm waiting to
see how the Lord leads," "I don't want to run ahead of God."
Such shibboleths rankle in the heart of the hard-driving
doer.

But the writer of Hebrews believes faith and patience do
belong together. So does the writer of Galatians ("The fruit of
the spirit is . . . patience . . . *faith*fulness . . . ."). Most Christians agree that salvation comes by faith, but whoever has
heard of being saved through patience? Salvation through
patience, however, is a subject the book of Hebrews explores
in depth. Written to Christians under fire, persecuted, hunted
and suffering defections in their weaker ranks, Hebrews urges
them to "hang in there" against all odds. Their eventual reward
will make every current setback seem worthwhile. Their persis-
tence (read "patience") will pay off. Their patience (read "faith
that will not let go no matter what") will save them.

Many years ago I preached a sermon on this same subject.
Some anonymous friend, who knew me well enough to doubt
my credentials for so presuming, went out that very afternoon,

bought a plaque, delivered it to my door and ran. I found it the gift but have never discovered the giver. It reads, "Lord, give me patience – but hurry!" To this day it hangs on the wall, a never-sleeping schoolmarm to scold me whenever my intolerance of delay approaches the boiling point.

Confession, as they say, is good for the soul, so I've told you how things are with me. It wasn't all that hard to admit it, because mine is not a unique flaw. As a matter of fact, our whole nation is similarly afflicted. You'd think, with all our electronic marvels and time-and labor-saving devices we'd have developed into a tranquil, steady-as-she-goes society. Instead we've migrated in the opposite direction. Ours is the most uptight culture ever.

Can you stand a little more computer talk? In the preceding chapter I disclosed my attachment to (no, my dependence on) the electronic notebook that is my constant companion. I refer to it as my "brains," its phenomenal storage capacity ("memory," we call it) supplementing my less reliable organic original. It is nearly indispensable to my work. Yet nothing in my adult life has exasperated me more than this infuriatingly logical machine. Technicians like to talk about the computer's programming, but anybody who uses the dictatorial instrument knows beyond doubt it's the computer that's in control and the operator that's programmed. You do what the computer tells you in exactly the way it commands, or it simply refuses to have anything to do with you.

If you are interested sometime in observing the fruit of the Spirit being squashed by an inanimate object, come watch me at the keyboard.

Misery loves company, so you can appreciate the glee with which I learn of other exasperated addicts. There was a sheriff in California who, when his computer started uncontrollably spewing out arrest records, simply drew out his revolver and shot it dead. He had my sympathy. In Minneapolis a computer pushed its operator too far. I don't know the offense, but the sentence was proper. He (or she, the culprit's identity is a secret) simply emptied a jar of honey into the works. Poetic justice.

I read of a New York computer that was murdered by a screwdriver. Less messy, but considerably noisier, than honey.

Your nemesis may not be the same as mine, but I suspect that you, too, experience moments of temporary insanity when "it" (whatever your "it" is) gets to you. If you do, then you will undoubtedly agree with Robert Schuller's maddeningly accurate assessment: "You're not defeated until you lose your patience."[1]

NOT losing your patience is what this chapter is about.

PATIENCE TO GROW

> Therefore let us leave the elementary teachings about Christ and go on to maturity, not laying again the foundation of repentance from acts that lead to death, and of faith in God, instruction about baptisms, the laying on of hands, the resurrection of the dead, and eternal judgment. And God permitting, we will do so . . . (Heb 6:1-3).

How easy to say, how hard to accept: Growth requires patience. For spiritual maturation, Hebrews urges getting on with it, growing beyond what initiates one into faith. Do the work at hand and stretch toward the tasks that lie ahead. Claiming to have been born again becomes a hollow boast if the reborn tarries indefinitely at the birthing place. Parents buttonhole their friends to exude over how rapidly their children are growing, not about how effectively they are prolonging their infancy.

In Hebrews the writer's irritation seeps through his sentences. He places no value on laying again the same foundation, in disputing endlessly about the basics, in reviewing again and again the teachings that first summoned belief. These are the legitimate concerns of a newcomer to the faith, not the maturing Christian.

Some persons find spiritual development difficult because of their timidity. They are afraid to grow, to venture. Others have an equally hard time because they try to jump-start their maturation. They are not accustomed to waiting for what they want. But some things can't be hurried. Spiritual maturation takes time; it builds step by step, experience on experience. You can't plant the eye of the potato tonight and expect it to provide your salted french fries for tomorrow's hamburger. Neither can you submit to baptism one day and take the reins of spiritual leadership the next. Or even the day after the next.

In my files are a few of my old sermons, reposing there as handy lessons in humility, lest I should ever forget. I blush to think of what those poor dear saints in that long-ago first church had to endure. Rereading those feeble efforts now makes me wonder what I'll think thirty years hence about the longsuffering saints listening to me today! In my case, personal spiritual growth has taken a very long time. It couldn't have been otherwise. I came to patience late in life.

Because there are so many of us spiritual "late-bloomers," patience with others as well as with ourselves is a grace without which church life cannot flourish. In any aggressively evangelistic congregation there will be believers at every level of maturity. The strong must be careful lest their impatience should drive out the weak. A toddling newborn's awkwardness will occasionally embarrass the old-timers in the faith, just as parents blush when their little ones misbehave in a friend's home. Recrimination is not the solution; generous portions of tolerance and loving nurture are.

I learned this lesson all over again when for several months our firstborn grandson and his parents lived with his grandmother and me. Kyle was just a toddler then. He made quite a study as he learned his way around on unsteady legs. His mother said I made an even more fascinating study. Kyle did terrible things to our apartment, upsetting this, spilling that, disrupting, misplacing – and I didn't ever get angry. He soiled the furniture, he dumped things on the carpet, and rearranged the placement of everything he could lift. In record time he undid his fastidious grandmother's best efforts at tidiness. If his mother, our daughter, had torn through the apartment with equally disastrous results, my reaction would have been immediate and vigorous, probably while pointing out that *her* mother needed to watch her more closely. That's not quite the truth. When Kim was Kyle's age, she was about as agile a destroyer as he, and her mother and I tolerated a great deal even then.

You see, even a person as short-tempered as I sometimes am can exercise almost infinite patience with toddlers. Why? Because they are doing the best they can for their years. They haven't had time to develop their coordination, judgment, social graces and sense of responsibility. We reasonably expect far less of toddlers than of adults.

Further reflection on the ways of the grandparent reveals something else: As my tolerance of Kyle's behavior is greater than for an adult's, so is it greater for a young adult than for myself. It takes time to grow through every phase of adulthood, too.

78

This double standard must be maintained in church as well as in family. In every vigorous congregation there are babies and parents and grandparents in the faith. Spiritual maturity isn't an instantaneous achievement. The waters of baptism don't release the candidates with the wisdom of sages; rather, they emerge rather with the freshness and ignorance of babies. At this point we now need Hebrews' warning against pushing my reasoning too far. You can tarry too long at the baptistry.

Some converts praise God they're "in." Forever after they can testify of the date and the hour of their conversion. They recount the details of their baptism, speaking in hushed tones as if it were an enchanted ritual which once performed perpetually fends off evil and ultimately delivers from hell. They're saved and satisfied. They grow no more.

The writer offers a corrective for this spiritual retardation, pleading for Christ's follows to get beyond the elementary things they have already mastered to a more fulfilling life. Drop back to the fifth chapter of Hebrews, to this warning in verse 11:

> We have much to say about this, but it is hard to explain because you are slow to learn. In fact, though by this time you ought to be teachers, you need someone to teach you the elementary truths of God's word all over again.

By now, believers, you ought to have outgrown the need for coddling. You still require milk when you ought to be on solid food:

> Anyone who lives on milk, being still an infant, is not acquainted with the teaching about righteousness.

The writer charges his readers to move beyond these "elementary things" which, surprisingly, include matters of conduct and doctrine that still dominate most church instruction, to right relationships with God and other people:

> But solid food is for the mature, who by constant use have trained themselves to distinguish good from evil.

What is required is the patience to discipline, and the discipline to stretch and stretch some more, even when exhausted.

Hebrews answers the long-time church member who grumbles "the preacher's not feeding us. There's no 'depth' in his messages." Is the problem with the feeder or the fed? What would you think of a public school pupil who stayed in the first grade year after year complaining his teacher was repeating the same old stuff? Wouldn't you encourage him to move up a grade, to accept a harder challenge, rather than to keep calling for new first grade teachers? If as a high school senior you find the instruction too simple, the best solution isn't to replace the instructor but to move yourself as quickly as possible on to college. And if in college the problem repeats itself, perhaps the fault doesn't lie in your professors but in the fact that you are now able to teach yourself without demanding that another spoon it out to you.

> In fact, though by this time you ought to be teachers, you need someone to teach you the elementary truths of God's word all over again.

To whom is he talking?

PATIENCE TO ABIDE

Some jobs are so important that, once having started them, you have to stay with them until they're finished. "If it's worth starting, it's worth finishing," Dad often informed me. The writer of Hebrews puts it a little differently:

> It is impossible for those who have once been enlightened, who have tasted the heavenly gift, who have shared in the Holy Spirit, who have tasted the goodness of the word of God and the powers of the coming age, if they fall away, to be brought back to repentance, because to their loss they are crucifying the Son of God all over again and subjecting him to public disgrace (Heb 6:4-6).

What makes one's restoration impossible? Fickleness. God has given his best; he can't offer anything finer than what's already been rejected. If that didn't satisfy, what will?

Staying power is lacking. What more can you expect of God? He has given his Holy Spirit, his Word, his power. If you turn away from him after all this, you demand too much and do too little. And probably – no, I must resist this temptation to soften the blow – and certainly, there isn't any hope of getting you back. That's what "impossible" means, isn't it?

Lloyd Ogilvie offers a helpful insight on the requisite staying power. "Patience is Christ's perspective on perplexities," he says. "In him we perceive the shortness of this life and the length of eternity."[2] Taking Christ's perspective brings out the vast difference between time's impermanence and eternity's foreverness. Who would exchange what you can't take with you for what can never be taken from you? Be patient. Don't quit too soon.

Early in my college teaching career our school's president taught me an unforgettable lesson in patience. He didn't know it. He wasn't overtly instructing on the principles of president-ing. He wasn't even conscious that class was being held. I was just making my own study, and he was the subject under exam-ination. Our president was seldom seen on campus. As a

81

fledgling professor I couldn't figure out what he did. He seemed to me almost superfluous to the operation. Things would go right on if he were there or if he weren't there. What exactly did he do? Did we really need him?

I discovered in time that we did indeed need him. As president, he filled two vital functions only he could perform. It became apparent that he was the one who must articulate the vision. And he must abide in office. In good times and bad, he had to "be there" for the college, reminding us who we were and what we were to do to fulfill the vision.

Later I asked Dr. Bruce Miller of our church staff, a former college president, whether he would add anything to my list. He didn't. He agreed that the president of a college or university must see the future for his institution and speak it into existence, not as God spoke the world into existence from nothing but as an effective academic leader persuades his college community to believe in and follow him into that future. Then he must stay with them long enough to get them there. He must abide.

Youth doesn't appreciate this need to persist. Instantaneous gratification is the pursuit of the young. They have no way of knowing personally how long it takes to plant and cultivate Christian virtues, how many years are required to comprehend what being a Christian is all about – to savor the rewards, the joys, the impact afforded by spiritual things.

Hence, according to Hebrews, once you've received these blessings of God, you must hang on to them. If you drop away, you'll lose them all. Sometimes you'll be tempted to give up. You feel so weak and the world seems so hostile. You will hurt; you'll lose heart. But if you know what's best for you, you'll hang on. If your family goes through a crisis (does any family escape them?) – death, job loss, a strained marriage, heartache over the children, trouble with the neighbors or relatives, whatever – hang on. Not very profound advice, I admit, but sometimes the wisest word is the simplest. Don't cut and run. Abide. Then one day, on the other side of the crisis, you'll relish the satisfaction of having stayed the course. Others may complain of burnout. Don't let them influence you. They will never know, as you will, the joy of your reward.

You can measure the values of a culture by studying its buzzwords. "Burnout" is one of today's most popular. You can attend seminars on how to avoid it, read books and articles analyzing it, and hear the malady complained of every time busy people congregate. Just a few years ago the word itself was unknown; today it almost seems that most of my acquaintances either are in it or one the brink of it. Who could have predicted that our era, with its plethora of labor-saving devices unimagined by our forerunners, would be the one to invent burnout?

A Sunday School teacher (who presents exactly one lesson a week!) thought she had come down with a severe case of it. She'd been teaching every Sunday without a break for a whole year, she wailed, and she couldn't take it any more. While she grumbled, I remembered the devoted teachers in my home church, many of whom had been at their posts for thirty, forty, and in one case, nearly fifty years. They didn't even know they could burn out. The word had to be invested before the excuse could be permitted.

Why do we give out so quickly? Don't you suspect it's because the other elements in the fruit of the Spirit are missing? Not knowing how to love, we haven't found joy and peace that come in doing what we love for those we love. Work without love degenerates into tedium, and nothing wears us out more quickly. My memory of those devoted Sunday School teachers of my youth is of women and men who deeply loved the Lord, their church, and the children they nurtured each week. They were convinced they were molding lives for the better. They couldn't conceive of doing anything more fulfilling. So they never burned out.

Talk to a mother of an invalid child, who cares for him through infancy and childhood and adolescence and into adulthood. Does she complain of burnout? Oh, she certainly grows weary, but that's a different thing. She still gets up the next morning and changes the bed linen and cleans the helpless body and spoons in the food and encourages each miniscule evidence of progress. Why? Because she loves.

My problem — and perhaps yours as well — is not impatience, you see. That's merely a symptom of the deeper malady, not *loving* enough. Having been taught to look out for ourselves, to take care of Number One first of all, we haven't the emotional and spiritual energy to love another as ourselves. So we rapidly sputter out, as a shallow wick soon flickers and dies because it does not draw from the source of light deep beneath it. How much better it is to become, to use the scriptural metaphor here, like rain-drenched land that produces.

PATIENCE TO PRODUCE

Land that drinks in the rain often falling on it and that produces a crop useful to those for whom it is farmed receives the blessing of God (Heb 6:7-8).

Productive, fruit-bearing lives receive God's blessing,

but land that produces thorns and thistles is worthless and is in danger of being cursed. In the end it will be burned . . . .

In John 15:16, Jesus also urges us to productivity:

You did not choose me, but I chose you and appointed you
to go and bear fruit – fruit that will last.

How shall we do it? As the soil does it, with patience. The
Apostle Paul names it a helpful quality in preaching and teaching:

Preach the Word; be prepared in season and out of season;
correct, rebuke and encourage – with great patience and careful
instruction (2 Tim 4:2).

Patience. The word seems to be everywhere. In the Russian
language there is an even stronger term, *priterpelost*. We
would translate it "servile patience," but servility is not what the
Scriptures have in mind. They do not urge us to put up with
the intolerable and certainly not with the unproductive. Biblical
patience is like the endurance of a woman in labor, who toler-
ates excruciating pain because she's producing. The patience of
an artist at his work is another example. He forgets to eat,
doesn't know what time it is, and can't be bothered by anything
else while he is producing.

Another personification of patience is the fisherman along a
river bank. You've probably guessed you won't find me standing with him. To a person of my temperament, fishing as a
sport seems an incredible waste of time, but dedicated fisher-
men disagree. They are anticipating their catch. They understand that before the catch comes the wait. They are waiting –
to produce.

I heard, incidentally, about a fisherman who could not be
used to illustrate my point. His reverie was interrupted by a fel-

low who had been watching him for awhile. "What are you doing?" he asked him.

"I'm fishing."

"But there aren't any fish in there."

"I know it."

"Then why are you fishing?"

"It's either this or my wife's got me working at home." In his case what appears to be patience is more likely mere laziness, and we've already concluded that the one is not to be confused with the other.

James first uses the farmer for comparison.

> Be patient, then, brothers, until the Lord's coming. See how the farmer waits for the land to yield its valuable crop and how patient he is for the autumn and spring rains. You too, be patient and stand firm, because the Lord's coming is near. Don't grumble against each other, brothers, or you will be judged. The Judge is standing at the door! (James 5:7-9).

Then he presents the prophet as a model:

> Brothers, as an example of patience in the face of suffering, take the prophets who spoke in the name of the Lord. As you know, we consider blessed those who have persevered. You have heard of Job's perseverance and have seen what the Lord finally brought about. The Lord is full of compassion and mercy (James 5:10, 11).

Be patient, then, about some things, but not everything. Don't grow complacent about sin or tolerant of injustice or satisfied with mediocrity. And don't let your church do it, either. A cartoon in our church's Sunday School paper *The Lookout* carried this dialogue:

First panel: "We could have built more Sunday School room but we waited for lower prices."

Second panel: "We could have enrolled many new members but

we waited for space to put them in."

Third panel: "Over the years we've watched our attendance drop far below what it used to be."

Fourth panel: "Sometimes I think patience is our biggest problem."

He's using the wrong word to describe the problem. Patience isn't the difficulty. Laziness is.

PATIENCE TO PERSEVERE AND INHERIT

> Even though we speak like this, dear friends, we are confident of better things in your case – things that accompany salvation. God is not unjust; he will not forget your work and the love you have shown him as you have helped his people and continue to help them (Heb 6:9-12).

God expects something of us. When we Christians exclaim with gratitude on our salvation by grace, we speak the truth, but not the whole truth. God's Word is crammed with commands, hints, suggestions, exhortations and demonstrations of what he expects his people to do. We know we're supposed to love God and love our neighbors. Many Scriptures, including the following one, tell us how to express that love.

> We want each of you to show this same diligence to the very end, in order to make your hope sure. We do not want you to become lazy, but to imitate those who through faith and patience inherit what has been promised (Heb 6:11,12).

Our Mesa congregation was blessed for many years by a saintly little lady named Maude Bailey. Until just a few weeks before her death she was in church every Sunday she could possibly get there, which was most of them, though she lived to be ninety-six years old. No one has encouraged and inspired me more in recent years. Reading these words in Hebrews I couldn't help thinking of her. She showed "this same diligence to the very end." Maude was old; she couldn't see or hear well. Walking was difficult; getting across our large parking lot and into the building was a challenge, yet she never arrived without her smile. She rose above every illness or challenge or dark mood. She wouldn't quit. Maude went to her grave without knowing how important her example was to many of us. She wasn't being diligent because she wanted to be an example; she was diligent because she understood such conduct to be what the Lord expects of all his children, whatever their ages. On those occasional days when the temptation to quit is so strong, remembering Maude never fails to shake me out of my self-pity. She was one of those "who through faith and patience inherit what has been promised."

Patience and *diligence* are not popular words, as we've already noted. Their ultimate reward, though, can't be claimed yet. It comes later.

We have to wait "to the very end" for what the Lord has promised. The waiting isn't passive, though, but a day by day expressing of faith in love, putting into practice what dare not be limited to words alone. The famous pianist, Paderewski, said one time, "If I miss a day of practice, I can tell a difference in my technique. If I miss two days, my wife also can note it. If I miss a week, even the public can tell."

Patient, diligent practice explains a pianist's mastery of technique. Patient, watchful readiness explains a statesman's ultimate triumph. West German Prime Minister Conrad Adenauer once explained his strategy for victory. "I believe patience is the strongest weapon in the armory of the defeated," he said, "and I possess a great deal of it. I can wait."

We also wait.

We wait upon the Lord.

And while we wait, we diligently do the will of him who will reward our *patience*, knowing that in the Lord we labor not in vain.

FOR YOUR FURTHER CONSIDERATION

1. Think a little longer about patience and laziness. Is the author a little too hard on "laid-back" personalities?

2. Do faith and patience belong together? Can you have one without the other?

3. Robert Schuller insists we're not defeated until we lose our patience. The author admits his computer has come close to defeating him. Do you have someone or something that particularly tries your patience? Who wins?

4. The author is at pains to remind the reader that maturation takes time; patience is required for spiritual growth. Why does he make this case at such great length?

5. How patient should we be with other people? With fellow Christians?

6. The writer of Hebrews warns that it's impossible to restore the Christian without staying power (a synonym for patience). What does he mean? Isn't the author a little unfair in his treatment of burnout? What's the best medicine for the condition?

8. Why do you think the apostle Paul includes a humble virtue like patience in a list that includes such major qualities as love, joy, and peace?

Endnotes

1. Robert Schuller, *Move Ahead with Possibility Thinking*. New York: Doubleday and Company, p. 174.
2. Lloyd Ogilvie, *Making Stress Work for You*. Waco: Word Books, 1984, p. 38.

KINDNESS ❧

Ephesians 2:6-8

"The fruit of the Spirit is love, joy, peace, patience,
kindness . . . ."

WE HAVE BEEN SAVED BY GRACE (KINDNESS)

Would you rather say you've been saved by God's *grace* or
by His *kindness*? Or by your *faith*? In Ephesians 2:6-8 Paul
uses all three expressions:

> And God raised us up with Christ and seated us with him in
> the heavenly realms in Christ Jesus, in order that in the coming
> ages he might show the incomparable riches of his *grace*,

expressed in his *kindness* to us in Christ Jesus. For it is by *grace* you have been saved, through *faith.*

Kindness is grace expressing itself.

When our new church building was under construction, the endless frustrations, delays and complications renewed my gratitude for God's having dealt kindly, faithfully, and graciously with us, and not legalistically. What a tangle of contradictory laws and regulations (euphemistically called building codes) we encountered. It seemed no matter how hard we tried to conform to the dictates of the laws, we were still guilty of some infraction or other. Doing what one inspector ordered brought us into conflict with another inspector. A recent remodeling job in California introduced me to the added frustrations of dealing with a general inspector who inspects the inspections of specific inspectors, like a policeman policing policemen. When we were finally about ready to move into our new church building in Arizona, one final absurdity stopped us. The fire inspector informed us we were in violation of the fire code. The letters on our main sign along the street were not large enough to be seen easily by the fire department. In case of fire, the firemen would need that help in locating our church. That sounds reasonable, you say, and it is, I suppose, except for the fact that the fire station is next door to the church.

I might as well tell you the rest of the story. On the side of our education building you will find a large number 8. Why? So that, in case of fire, the fire department will know precisely which building on the church campus is burning. Probably only two or three persons in our congregation know that it's Building Number 8, but somewhere in the files of the firehouse there must be a map of our property with a building boldly marked #8. I have fun imagining firemen in a truck tooling onto our campus, the driver yelling, "Where's Building Number 8?" and our 3,000 members looking at one another in puzzlement. Complying with that code will only confuse everybody if we ever have an actual emergency. But the law must be obeyed, no matter how absurd it is.

If you've been in the building business, you know about these frustrations. I'm not trying to find fault with anybody at city hall or in the fire department. Codes and regulations and laws are necessary to prevent anarchy. But wherever there is law, there will be legalism, violation, sin and guilt, since we inevitably run afoul of its demands.

Trying to live in compliance with just the building code, let alone the city ordinances and county regulations and state and federal laws, and failing regularly, offers proof enough that satisfying a God of Law would be impossible. When Paul writes, "It is for freedom that Christ has set us free [from the *law* of sin and death]," every liberated Christian rejoices. There's hope after all.

What an amazing kindness God did us.

Kindness is not a word we ordinarily associate with what God accomplished through Christ. We use it more readily to describe commendable social behavior: "Be ye kind one to another," our childhood teachers intoned.

Some time ago I read the autobiography of Moss Hart, one of America's best-known playwrights. He had collaborated with the famous George Kaufmann on a play, and, on the opening night, was amazed to see Kaufmann, who had always ridiculed authors who went up to take their bows on opening night, ascend the stage steps to speak. What he had to say further shocked Hart. When the audience grew quiet the older man said very simply, "I would like this audience to know that eighty

percent of this play is Moss Hart's." The crowd was disappointed; they had expected a witty speech in Kaufmann's inimitable
style. But Hart had tears in his eyes. Who could have expected
the much more renowned playwright so graciously to honor his
younger collaborator? Especially since, as Hart describes the
reciprocal animosities of the theatrical world, "Few are uncor-
rupted by its ceaseless warfare over credit and billing, its jeal-
ousies and envies, its constant temptations toward pettiness
and mean-spiritedness."[1]

Don't you wish Hart's indictment could be limited to the the-
ater? Could he have written the same of your sphere or mine? I
sadly confess I know of no profession, no occupation or trade,
no group of any kind meeting anywhere of whom it could be
reported, "They are never petty; they are never mean-spirited;
they never fight over who gets the credit."

What causes this sad situation? Whether at home, on the
job, in the neighborhood or wherever, there is within us some
insecurity or egocentricity – call it what you want –that seeks
the glory. And glory-seeking and kindness do not keep one
another company.

Given this innate propensity toward self-promotion, Jesus'
incomparable gift seems all the more extraordinary. Paul
describes us precisely: "As for you, you were dead in your
transgressions and sins . . . ." We didn't deserve anything good
from God, yet not only have we received His grace (kindness),
we have been saved by it. What then does he want from us?

> For we are God's workmanship, created in Christ Jesus to
> do good works, which God prepared in advance for us to do
> (Eph 2:10).

He has been gracious to us so that we, in turn, may be gracious to others through doing good works. God's divine kindness, he hopes, will come to characterize us.

The prophet Jeremiah, speaking for the Lord, says:

> But let him who boasts boast about this: that he understands and knows me, that I am the Lord who exercises kindness, justice and righteousness on earth, for in these I delight, declares the Lord (9:24).

The Lord delights in "kindness, justice and righteousness." Jesus offers us the best advice for learning these virtues in the verse we call the Golden Rule:

> So in everything, do to others what you would have them do to you . . . . (Matt 7:12).

Can you think of a better rule for one who wants to learn kindness?

In the early days of computer technology, a story circulated of a great super-computer, one unlike any that had ever been seen. Having fed it the wisdom of all the ages, its creators had assembled a group of the world's greatest living intellectuals draw straws for the privilege of challenging it. An old poet drew the winning straw. His question has burdened all the world's deep thinkers: "What is the true way to bring brotherhood and harmony to all mankind?" The collected human minds waited as the electronic brain ran through its storehouse of data (it took longer in those days) and then spit out its answer: "Each must perpetrate upon all others only that which he would find agreeable and beneficial if perpetrated upon himself." The Golden Rule, in computerese.

One of the great American exemplars of the Golden Rule ethic was Abraham Lincoln, who frequently spoke with kindness of the Southern states even during the heat of battle. On one such occasion, an elderly woman accosted him in the reception room of the White House. "How can you speak kindly of your enemies," she asked him, "when you should rather destroy them?" President Lincoln said, "But, madam, do I not destroy them when I make them my friends?"[2]

Lincoln's wartime compassion embodies the spirit of the apostles. In Acts 3 and 4, for example, Peter and John, on their way to the temple to pray, are accosted by a beggar, as common an occurrence then as it is now at most of the world's holy places. The man has been crippled all his life and has been carried daily to the temple to beg, since he cannot work for a living. The disciples look him in the eye, raising his anticipation level. They can't give him what he wants; instead, they offer something far superior.

"Silver and gold I don't have, but what I have, I give you," Peter tells him. "In the name of Jesus Christ of Nazareth walk."

And he does.

The miracle raises a ruckus, of course, and Peter and John have to defend themselves before the Supreme Court of the Jews, the Sanhedrin. Peter's language bears a close look:

"Rulers and elders of the people! If we are being called to account today for an act of *kindness* to a cripple and are asked how he was healed, then know this, you and all the people of Israel: It is by the name of Jesus Christ of Nazareth, whom you crucified but whom God raised from the dead, that this man stands before you healed."

"An act of kindness," Peter calls it, as if to say, "We merely offered what we had to give. We did what we could, that's all." You and I may not have the apostle's gift of healing, but we aren't without our own God-given resources. The gift may be money, or labor, or simply our caring presence, but we are always able to offer some "act of kindness."

A review of Romans 12:6f will be helpful here, especially if you have wondered what kindness you can offer.

> We have different gifts, according to the grace given us. If a man's gift is prophesying, let him use it in proportion to his faith. If it is serving, let him serve; if it is teaching, let him teach; if it is encouraging, let him encourage; if it is contributing to the needs of others, let him give generously; if it is leadership, let him govern diligently; if it is showing mercy, let him do it cheerfully.

Tempted to discount our abilities if we can't do the showy things like healing, teaching, singing, speaking, we need this passage's wise leveling of up-in-front and behind-the-stage services. They are equally valuable. Look at the list again.

First Paul names preaching (prophesying), an attention-getting gift. But the very next one he mentions is serving, which never calls attention to itself but is essential in the Body of Christ. Then comes another up-front activity, teaching, which is again quickly coupled with encouraging and contributing and mercy-giving, all of which are quietly offered behind the scenes and are within the capacity of just about everybody. Kindness, of which these gifts are expressions, is definitely within everyone's reach.

Never discount your importance, then, especially if your gift is one of the quiet but essential ones. I often think of my indebtedness to many servants in our church on Sunday morning, when I stand at the pulpit. The main room of our meeting house is designed in a half-circle, with the pulpit at the axis, all the seats facing it. It's a dangerous design; unless he exercises caution, the speaker can entertain delusions of grandeur. He can get the idea that his role is more important than that of others. If one of the sound technicians misses a Sunday, however, the whole congregation learns quickly what an indispensable servant he is.

As the speaker, I am offering what I can give. Members of the congregation, offering their service of listening, are doing the same. They are encouraging. One some occasions, no doubt, they are offering mercy through the practice of endurance. You think I jest. Do you have any idea what it's like to have to keep on speaking after people have quit listening? Such is the stuff of nightmares. As a matter of fact, my two worst nightmares are that I have forgotten to put on my trousers before preaching, or that as I'm preaching the congregation gets up and walks out. Believe me when I tell you how grateful I am for the the kindness of consecrated saints who listen. They are giving what they have to offer – and this preacher can't thank them enough.

How essential is the kindness of those who "only" listen. I once had a professor in a graduate course at East Tennessee State University who understood this. He announced we would not be meeting for the next scheduled class because he would be attending his professional meeting in another city. We were impressed, believing he would be reading a paper before his colleagues. "Oh, no," he corrected us. They have to have somebody to read to. I'm going to listen." That moment I realized as never before how important that little service of listening is. Having always focused on the podium, I hadn't fully appreciated those who "merely" listen, who encourage, and if need be, who show mercy.

Because my career is a talking one, I've arbitrarily selected listening as the example. Listeners have been kind to me. They represent all kind persons whose importance is far greater than any reward they can ever expect from those they serve. These are the people Jesus had in mind when He said, "You are the salt of the earth . . . the light of the world." Without the kindness of such persons, what would this world be?

Henrietta Mears, for many years the dynamic Minister of Christian Education at Hollywood Presbyterian Church, influenced dozens of young men for the ministry. I learned something of her secret of success when I read that she said, "Every time I meet someone," she said, "I visualize a sign across their chest which says, 'My name is ____. Please help me feel important.'"[4]

Everybody wants to feel important. Surely the Spirit expects us to treat all people as if they really are, which is the inescapable lesson the Gospel teaches. You've never seen such a sign, but you've seen that hope in people's eyes, haven't you? Who doesn't need to be encouraged? It's a simple gesture of kindness to grant their request, isn't it? It isn't hard, either, especially when you make up your mind that kindness will be your lifestyle, courtesy your everyday habit.

"But I don't know what to say," you might tell me.

"Then don't say anything," I will answer. The secret of kindness isn't in your speaking, remember, but in your listening, your caring, your attending.

Most of the time you don't have to say anything, which is the point Keith Miller makes in his recounting of the visits friends made when his father died. He wanted to cry but couldn't, so he busied himself serving coffee, helping the guests. When almost everybody had left, their condolences offered, one man remained behind. He had spent the entire evening sitting at the end of the couch, speaking little. Only after the other guests had departed did Keith really notice him, a nearby rancher, holding his Stetson hat in his lap. He stood, walked over to Keith and said, "Son, I knew your daddy and he was a fine man." Then, looking him in the eye and shaking his hand, he turned around and left.

> "I've never forgotten that man," Keith Miller adds, "and I can't remember anybody else who came to call that night. The fact that he came and sat with us in our grief all evening without having to say a thing, then finally made a comment about my dad and left was enough. That man had come for my father and for us. I can't even remember his name, but his presence had an enormous effect on me."[5]

Joy and I heard almost the same story when we flew from Arizona to Portland after our "adopted" grandson's fatal motor- cycle accident. Shawn's father told us about his friend who, like the rancher, just came and sat. He, too, didn't know what to say or how to say it. Of all the sympathizers who came by the house in those days after the accident, the one whose kindness spoke most eloquently to Jeff was his inarticulate friend John. (Jeff and Joan had equal praise for John's wife, who tackled the dishes, provided food, and helped in a dozen unobtrusive ways to ease them through their days. Kindness comes in many forms.)

Kindness is not something you buy at a store and wrap in sil- ver paper. It is, more than anything else, a portion of yourself offered in love. Your presence is often enough – more valuable by far than anything you can purchase.

Let me conclude this meditation with a very well-known story of an old doctor in a village in France who had cared for his people for fifty years. Night and day he was at their dispos- al, delivering their babies, comforting their aged, nursing their afflicted. But the inevitable day came when he had to announce his retirement. A grateful town council declared a day of celebration for their doctor. As a gift to him, each family in the village was to bring one cup of their finest wine to be presented on behalf of them all. So before the appointed time, a representative from each family secretly poured a cupful into the beautiful wooden cask the village was giving to their beloved benefactor.

The big day arrived. Orations were delivered, glowing tributes to the man's beneficence. The doctor was asked to draw a cup of wine. He did as instructed, but instead of drawing a cup of fine wine, he drew water. Each villager, presuming all others would bring their best, thought one cup of water among so much wine would never be noticed. The old doctor stood up, tears forming in his eyes as he looked around at the people he had so kindly served for half a century. He smiled a sad smile and without saying a word, made his way out of the crowd.

Thus was his kindness repaid.

"By his grace you have been saved."

How are you repaying the *kindness*?

FOR YOUR FURTHER CONSIDERATION

1. Which *are* we saved by, grace, kindness or faith?

2. Why are kind persons so rare? In this "dog-eat-dog" world, is it possible for a kind person to get ahead?

3. You know the Golden Rule. What rule does today's society live by?

4. Is Abraham Lincoln's the most effective way of destroying your enemies? How does it work?

5. Of the gifts listed in Romans 12, which ones do you deem to be most important? Why?

6. The author praises the kindness of listening because he is a speaker. What expression of kindness is especially important to you? Why? What expression are you best equipped to offer?

7. What is the best way for you to make another person feel important?

8. What makes the gift of one's presence so valuable to another person, especially in times of bereavement?

9. This chapter says very little about the role of the Holy Spirit in helping us to be kind to one another. Do you know any particular Scripture that says so, or is that help to be assumed? In other words, why is kindness named among the other virtues that constitute the fruit of the Spirit?

Endnotes

1. Moss Hart, *Act One, an Autobiography.* New York: Vintage, 1959, p. 369.

2. Carl Sandburg, Abraham Lincoln: *The War Years,* Volume 3. New York: Harcourt, Brace and Company, 1939, pp. 495, 496.

3. "Encouragement," *Christian Leadership Letter,* Published by World Vision, November 1983.

4. Keith Miller and Bruce Larson, *Carriers of the Spirit: The Passionate People.* Waco: Word Books, 1979, p. 42.

GOODNESS 🔖

2 Peter 1:3-7

"The fruit of the Spirit is love, joy, peace, patience, kindness, *goodness* . . . ."

His divine power has given us everything we need for life and godliness through our knowledge of him who called us by his own glory and *goodness*. Through these he has given us his very great and precious promises, so that through them you may participate in the divine nature and escape the corruption in the world caused by evil desires. For this very reason, make every effort to add to your faith *goodness*; and to *goodness*, knowledge; and to knowledge, self-control; and to self-control, perseverance; and to perseverance, godliness; and to godliness, brotherly kindness; and to brotherly kindness, love.

103

GOD HAS GIVEN . . .

This Scripture begins where we always must begin – with what God has already given us, which is "everything we need for life and godliness." As far as the Bible is concerned, the only real, worthwhile life is a godly one. God, the Source of goodness, has provided all we require through Jesus, who called us, not because of our deserving, but because that's who he is and what he does.

The Psalmist agrees:

How great is *your* goodness,
    which you have stored up for those who fear you,
which you bestow in the sight of men
    on those who take refuge in you (Ps 31:19).
But you, O Sovereign Lord,
    deal well with me for *your* name's sake;
out of the goodness of *your* love,
    deliver me (Ps 109:21).

Deliverance does not depend on our presenting ourselves to God as exemplary human beings, an impossibility anyway, but on his matchless character. Do you share my astonishment at the presumption of the person who boasts, in one way or another, "Sure, I'm going to heaven. I'm one of the good ones"? I always want to ask, "Good by whose standards? How do you express it, this goodness of yours? How come I haven't recognized it in you? Why did you have to tell me? Shouldn't it be apparent? Shouldn't it somehow look like God's goodness?"

Today's popular pop-psychologies and quasi-theologies boosting self-esteem may be relatively harmless, so long as we don't take them too seriously. When they lead to personal definitions of goodness and then to congratulating ourselves on our commendable attainment of these substandard goals, however, they betray us. If there is a God in heaven and if it is indeed he who sets the universal criteria of right and wrong, good and evil, and further, if it is he who will render final judgment, then self-advertised goodness will go for naught. It is far better, rather, to go to the Source to seek the saving goodness.

To speak of goodness as the Spirit's fruit is to acknowledge that this prized characteristic is not of our own doing. Scriptures leave no room for misunderstanding: we are sinners who, in spite of ourselves, have received God's grace through Jesus Christ. By *his* goodness we were saved, through *his* goodness we are supported, to *his* goodness we aspire, and on *his* Spirit we depend. Our only valid boast is about the One who blesses and improves us. As recipients of God's goodness, we seek appropriate ways to thank him. Even to do that we rely on his Spirit.

GOD WANTS OF US . . .

How can I repay the Lord
    for all his goodness to me? (Ps 116:12).

2 Peter answers the question the Psalmist raises:

Through these he has given us his very great and precious promises, so that through them you may participate in the divine nature and escape the corruption in the world caused by evil desires (2 Pet 1:4).

God not only wants us to be like him but he makes it possible.

The challenge, to be sure, is to escape this world's corruption. What makes the flight so fearsome is that the enemy we flee isn't somewhere out there in the seductive world so much as in here, in our "evil desires." These urges are so powerful and pervasive we are forced to define good behavior negatively, as *not* doing certain things, as in those lines my home church preacher used to quote:

> "I don't smoke
> and I don't chew
> and I don't go
> with the girls who do."

Therefore I'm a good person!
Sorry, such barren goodness isn't good enough.

GOD WANTS US TO
PARTICIPATE IN HIS DIVINE NATURE

God's goodness is active, involved. You've seen those little statues of the Buddha. They're almost always identical in mood: passive, smiling, unsympathetic, self-contained. He's the antithesis of the active, emotive, sympathetic, other-directed God of the Bible, who creates and guides and rescues and scolds and feeds and loves. He snatches his people from slavery in Egypt, settles them in a promised land, suffers their rebellions, heals their wounds, hears their prayers, suffers their provocations and never forsakes them. He is the God who reveals himself in Christ Jesus, who is himself the personification of goodness. In Jesus goodness heals the epileptic, makes the lame to walk again, restores sight to the blind and hope to the desperate. In Jesus goodness makes the ultimate sacrifice. Because of Jesus, goodness can only be fully described with reference to a cross.

To speak of God's divine nature, then, is not to conjure up

an inactive, aloof, inert God, but one who is doing – and doing good – for people.

Goodness thus is not to be defined negatively, by what is not done, but positively. To be good is to be good for something (anybody can be good for nothing); more accurately, it is to be good for somebody. Good persons are not only admirable in themselves; they become forces for good on behalf of others. Further, they are stimulants of goodness in others, for this spiritual trait is as contagious in its own way as evil is in its. Goodness breeds goodness.

Making my way from the North American Christian Convention hall toward my hotel in Oklahoma City a few years ago, I was stopped by a voice from behind. Turning around, I immediately recognized the very large young man from the past who towered above me (I tend to remember people over 6'4"), a former student. He had hailed me so he could bring me up to date on a little deal we had transacted twenty years earlier. I had forgotten about it.

"You'll remember me as a student having a difficult time financially," he said. "You gave me money to keep me going. You said at the time there was a family in Oregon that was sending you money to help needy students. When you gave me the money, you said I couldn't pay it back but that some time I could pay it on. I just want you to know that this last year I was able to pay it on, and I made the same speech to a struggling student as the one you made to me."

Then the memories came flooding back. It had been many years since I had thought about my special mission. When I resigned my pastorate in Oregon to become a professor at Milligan College in Tennessee, an older couple (about the age Joy and I are now – but they seemed much older, somehow) whom

107

I had been able to help on a couple of occasions (they were not members of our church) came to see me with this proposition: "When you're back there at that college, we're going to send you money from time to time to help students who are in financial difficulty. Don't let them pay it back; just tell them to pay it on."

You can imagine the great fun I had distributing their checks. We had our share of poverty-stricken students in those days. These unsolicited gifts made a big difference. Their benefactors were not wealthy people. Their checks were small and we were able to make a significant difference to only a few students, but every time I handed over some money, I explained its source and their donors' insistence that they not try to pay it back but to wait for an opportunity later to pass it on. When this outstanding teacher stood on that Oklahoma City sidewalk and recounted what he had done, it was the first report I had received that someone had kept the goodness flowing, two decades later.

This is exactly how God's economy works. His call to Abram makes his expectations explicit:

> I will make you into a great nation
>   and *I will bless you*
> I will make your name great,
>   and *you will be a blessing.*
> I will bless those who bless you,
>   and whoever curses you I will curse;
> and all peoples on earth
>   will be blessed through you (Gen 12:2, 3).

God blesses to bless. Those who receive his favor are to be conduits through which the goodness can flow to others. He doesn't want direct repayment. How could we repay him, anyway? But we can pay the blessings on, becoming in the act a little bit like God.

Actively doing good invites risks. He who forfeited his sanctuary in the heavens to walk among us deliberately contaminated himself. He consorted with sinners. He felt our hunger pangs. He sagged with our exhaustion. He was subjected to our temptations. He became like one of us, a risky venture, for which he paid dearly. There's something daring about goodness.

An inner-city Chicago minister had to face up to it in a hurry one day. When he answered his telephone, an agitated voice blurted out,

"Does anyone in your church have AIDS?"

The minister gave his time-tested response: "Why do you ask?"

The man wouldn't be stalled. "I visited your church Sunday morning and I read in your bulletin – you know, that bit that says, 'Anyone interested in helping to draft an official church policy statement regarding AIDS,' and then it says where to meet." Then he repeated himself, "I want to know if anyone in your church has AIDS. Do you think anyone with AIDS shook hands with me Sunday morning?"

I applaud Dennis Sawyer's answer. "Sir, in a city as large as Chicago, you probably encounter someone every day who has been exposed to the AIDS virus." He tried to explain to the man that there was no danger of getting AIDS from non-sexual contact. Then he added, "Sir, in any large church in this city, you will probably find people who have been exposed to the AIDS virus."

Then I'll stay home and watch TV," he growled, and slammed the receiver.[1]

109

This exchange forced me to think of the church I serve. Our average worship attendance is 3,000, twice the size of my wife's home town. How would I answer the question? I could truthfully say I don't know of anybody in our church who has AIDS, but I suspect that among three thousand people somebody does. Certainly there are carriers of the virus. What do we do about it? More specifically, what do we do about those persons? Shun them? Expel them? Make them shout, "Unclean!"

I more than suspect that among our members is at least one who is caught up in some sin or other. Maybe several. What do we do about them? Shun them? Expel them? Confine them to colonies of their kind to protect the rest of us from them?

This is no hypothetical case I'm posing here. This sort of thing has happened to me, the first time as a fledgling youth director. In checking with Cal Jernigan, our youth minister, I learned it's happened to him as well. The phone rings, and the angry voice of an irate parent announces, "I'm pulling my kid out of your youth group. You're letting the wrong kinds of young people in. I don't want my son/daughter hanging out with bad influences. Either they go, or my kid goes."

What should we do? Promise to limit our youth group to "good" young people only, sinners need not apply? What about us adults? Should we advertise that only righteous persons need visit, sinners being unwanted here? From time to time I remind the members of our flock that if a church is doing its evangelistic job, if it is reaching out to the people the Lord came to rescue, and if it is participating in the divine nature of God, then in that body will be people at every stage of spiritual development, including zero. A congregation embracing only good people is a bad church.

What do we do? Maybe a little lesson from my father would

help you, as it helped me. He used himself as an example to encourage me when I was a teenager. Dad didn't drink, but all his friends did. He smiled as he recollected those days. "The parents of my friends were always glad when they heard that I was going to the party, because they knew that Verne would be able to drive their kids home." He didn't parade his virtue and he didn't shun his friends. He quietly lived a notch above their standard. He could be with them without feeling he had to do everything they did. His parents didn't refuse permission for him to associate with young people who weren't "as good as" he was. They knew he was a responsible person, what we'd call a good kid.

I couldn't help wondering how many lives his goodness saved.

GOD WANTS US TO ESCAPE THE
CORRUPTION IN THE WORLD CAUSED BY EVIL DESIRES

> For you were once darkness, but now you are light in the Lord. Live as children of light (for the fruit of the light consists in all goodness, righteousness and truth) and find out what pleases the Lord (Eph 5:8-10).

Jesus said of himself, "I am the light of the world" (John 9:5).

The purpose of his coming was not to curse the darkness (there had been cursing enough, even back then), but to be a source of enlightenment, a way through and out of the darkness. Further, he provided for a perpetual flame to blaze, so that in succeeding generations no one should have to be lost in the darkness. To his disciples he gave the charge: "You (now) are the light of the world" (Matt 5:14).

111

Again we notice the scriptural motif: we receive in order to give. Having been enlightened by the Light of the world, we become like candles piercing the darkness. He who saved us now calls us to save others.

A good friend and member of our congregation visited the Soviet Union just months before its demise. Lee Barte spent three weeks there as a consultant in water management. When I asked him what he learned, his answer startled me. He said he had learned that 3.5 million people are going to die because of Chernobyl, the nuclear power meltdown.

"Three and a half million, Lee?" I thought I had misunderstood him.

Yes," he said, "and that many more will be permanently maimed."

After our conversation I read up a little more about Chernobyl, a tragedy that didn't have to happen. A series of bad decisions by people covering up their mistakes caused the meltdown. They didn't really want millions of people killed or maimed; they weren't "bad" people, we would say. They were just looking out for themselves. If others got hurt because of their selfishness, too bad, but they had to look out for themselves, didn't they?

Stock the world with people looking out primarily for themselves and you cover the earth with darkness. What such a world needs now is light. In Christ, God gave the light: you and I, on whom the light has shone, are reflectors of that light. For that reason,

GOD WANTS US TO ADD TO OUR VIRTUES

. . . make every effort to add to your faith goodness; and to

112

goodness, knowledge; and to knowledge, self-control; and to self-control, perseverance; and to perseverance, godliness; and to godliness, brotherly kindness; and to brotherly kindness, love (2 Pet 1:5-7).

Why?

For if you possess these qualities in increasing measure, they will keep you from being ineffective and unproductive in your knowledge of our Lord Jesus Christ (2 Pet 1:8).

"The fruit of the spirit is . . . goodness." How do we produce such fruit? As usual, through the little things that mean a lot. When I was a teenager, there was a popular song of that title: "Little Things Mean a Lot." I've forgotten the song, but not the lesson. Henry Kissinger, writing on the effective use of power in the White House, found the difference between success and failure was not in anything big but in what he called the "accumulation of nuances," the hundreds of little things done a little better. In politics as in everything else, little things mean a lot. We can be more productive, effective Christians by doing good things better.

Charles Colson, the dynamic head of Prison Fellowship, puts this into perspective by telling of his visit in Columbus, Georgia, to ninety-one-year-old Myrtie Howell, in her dilapidated nursing home in the center of town. He found the outside of the building depressing and the inside even more so. Residents dozed in the hallways; others stared blankly at nothing. The place stank of sickness and death – until the moment he stepped into Myrtie's room. Thrilled to meet him, Myrtie greeted him from her rocking chair, in which she sat like a queen on her throne. Her little domicile was far from palatial, though; smaller than an average hotel room, it held a bed, a twelve-inch television set, a little dresser, a mirror plastered with photos of prisoners, several chairs, and a fragile desk piled high with Bibles and commentaries and lots of letters.

Myrtie Howell had lived a hard life. She was born in Texas in 1890; her family moved to Georgia when she was three. She had been given only one year of school. When she was ten, she began working in a mill for ten cents a day. Married at seventeen, she gave birth to her first child at eighteen, then, in rapid succession, bore two more. The middle one died when he was only two. Then her husband was killed in an accident. So this humble woman, without education or career skills, slaved to rear her remaining two children. Finally, when her frail body couldn't work any more, she moved into what she called "this old folks home." She prayed to die but also asked, "Lord, what more can I do for You? If You're ready for me, I'm ready to come. I want to die. Please take me."

She believed she was dying when she became convinced the Lord had spoken. He said, "WRITE TO PRISONERS."

"Imagine that! I want to die, figure I'm about to, and the Lord say, 'Okay now, Myrtie, you go back and write to prisoners.'"

She didn't know any prisoners; she didn't know how to start. So she stalled. "Lord, me write to prisoners? I ain't got no education, had to teach myself to read and write. And I don't know nuthin' bout prisons." But she did know what to do when the Lord speaks.

She addressed her first letter to Atlanta Penitentiary, Atlanta, Georgia:

> Dear Inmate, I'm a grandmother who love and care for you who are in a place you had not plans to be.
> My love and sympathy goes out to you. I'm willing to be a

friend to you in correspondent.

If you'd like to hear from me, write me. I will answer every letter you write.

A Christian friend,
Grandmother Howell

The letter was passed on to the chaplain, who sent her names of eight prisoners. Her correspondence ministry had begun. In time she was writing to forty prisoners at a time. The number eventually totaled into the hundreds. She read Chuck Colson some of her answers, a sentence from this one and another from that one:

> Dear Grandmother . . . was very happy to get your letter . . . the guys kidded me when they said I had a letter . . . I didn't believe them, but it was true. I don't have anyone to care about me but the Lord and you . . . I'm in the hole now, that's why I can write letters . . . Why am I so afraid, grandmother? Why doesn't God answer my prayers about this? . . . I am really glad to know there is someone out there who cares . . . I will remember you in my prayers every night starting now for the rest of my life . . . please write back soon . . . love, Joe . . . in the love of Jesus, David . . .

She let Chuck read the entire letter from Granddaughter Janice:

> Dear Grandmother,
>
> I received your letter and it made me sad when you wrote that you think you may not be alive much longer. I thought I would wait and come to see you and then tell you all you have meant to me, but now I've changed my mind. I'm going to tell you now.
>
> You've given me all the love and concern and care that I've missed for years and my whole outlook on life has changed. You've made me realize that life is worth living and that it's not all bad. You claim it's all God's doing but I think you deserve

115

the credit.

I didn't think I was capable of feeling love for anyone again but I know now I love you as my very own precious grandmother.

Chuck Colson said as he walked out of the building he once again passed by the people sitting and staring.

> There was no joy in any of their expressions. Instead, their sunken eyes seemed to reflect a raging anger: anger that their families had left them there; anger that fate had dealt them cruel blows; anger that their minds were weak and their bones brittle; anger that their favorite TV program was interrupted or that someone else was served ahead of them at lunch.

He had originally gone to see Grandmother Howell because he had received this letter:

"Please pray for Grandma Howell cause she's sick and may be going to die. Nobody has ever loved me like she has. I just wait for her letters, they mean so much."

While he was visiting her, Myrtie Howell told him, "Writing to inmates has filled my last days with joy." She asked Colson to have her funeral. She said, "It won't help me but it will wake up my church to the need of taking part in prison ministry."[2]

Do you see how goodness passes on and elicits more goodness? And how important the little things are – things like writing a few letters?

Look around. All around you are people starving for goodness. Their world has been brutalized by selfishness. They protect themselves behind hard, sometimes threatening but not impenetrable facades. Their defenses can be pierced, their fears assuaged, and their darkness turned to light. But it will take somebody's goodness to do it.

Perhaps yours.

So "make every effort to add to your faith . . . *goodness.*"

FOR YOUR FURTHER CONSIDERATION

1. How do you know whether or not you are a good person? What constitutes goodness?

2. What does goodness have to do with our salvation? Whose goodness?

3. Have you ever received some act of goodness which you could not repay? Did you pass it on?

4. Why does God bless us?

5. The author writes, "Actively doing good invites risks." What kind of risks? Can they be avoided?

6. What can we do to guarantee that all the members of our churches are good people?

7. What recommendation would you give a young Christian who wanted to add to his faith goodness?

Endnotes

1. "An Aids Policy: Two Churches' Search," *Leadership Magazine*, Spring 1988, p. 96.
2. Charles Colson, *Loving God*. Grand Rapids: Zondervan, 1983, pp. 209-216.

FAITHFULNESS ❧

Psalm 89:1, 2, 14

"The fruit of the Spirit is love, joy, peace, patience, kindness, goodness, *faithfulness* . . . ."

Fifty-nine times the word *faithfulness* appears in the Bible.
Three verses from the 89th Psalm showcase it:

> I will sing of the Lord's great love forever;
>> with my mouth I will make your *faithfulness* known
>>> through all generations.
>
> I will declare that your love stands firm forever,
>> that you established your faithfulness in heaven itself.
>
> Righteousness and justice are the foundation of your
>> throne;
>> love and faithfulness go before you.

Most of the 59 times, the word is used in reference to God. This desirable virtue in the Spirit-filled believer can best be appreciated by observing how God exhibits it. The Psalms are especially helpful.

Much Hebrew poetry is written in parallel lines. The poet states something in one line and then in the next repeats his meaning in other words, as in the verses above. Look at the first line again.

I will sing of the *love* of the Lord forever.

Now look at the second one:

With my mouth I will make your *faithfulness* known through all generations.

Do you see the parallels?

sing = with my mouth
love = faithfulness
Lord = your
forever = through all generations

FAITHFULNESS IS LOVE HANGING ON

In one of his most popular songs, Frank Sinatra used to acclaim the unity of "love and marriage," which "go together like a horse and carriage." "You can't have one without the other," he crooned. Neither can you speak of love without implying faithfulness. The Psalmist treats them as synonymous. In this verse, faithfulness is love so constant he can sing of it forever.

In the 92nd Psalm the same praise is uttered in a slightly different way:

120

> It is good to praise the Lord
>> and make music to your name, O Most High,
> to proclaim your *love* in the morning
>> and your *faithfulness* at night . . . .(vss. 1, 2).

What is love in the morning becomes faithfulness at night. You have probably already memorized Psalm 100:5:

> For the Lord is good and his *love* endures forever,
> his *faithfulness* continues through all generations.

Once again love and faithfulness are coupled. Actually, nobody has to tell us they go together. We frequently equate them in our relationships. How can you tell whether I love you? Only by my faithfulness. Always. "I love you" is a pledge of allegiance.

Faithfulness doesn't wander, isn't fickle, won't quit. Sissela Bok quotes her mother's adage that "it's not worthy of human beings to give up," no matter what the battle.[1] My parents said the same thing a little differently. <u>Anything worth starting is worth finishing</u>, they repeated so often I've never been able to forget the lesson.

It's a good one. Quitters are impossible to admire. We value stick-to-it-iveness precisely because it requires strength of character. Having tried it and found ourselves wanting, we sympathize with Martin Luther's prayer:

> Dear Lord,
> Although I am sure of my position,
> I am unable to sustain it without Thee.
> Help Thou me, or I am lost.[2]

Lost because without faithfulness I am unworthy of my Lord; lost because without my Lord I am incapable of faithfulness. It's not sufficient to begin the day with a cheery, "Good morning, Lord. Starting this morning, I'm going to be faithful. You can count on it. I admit I let you down yesterday, and the day before that, and yes, before that one, too. But today's different. You'll see." Morning's resolutions can't resist evening's temptations. As Mark Twain put it, "Habit is . . . not to be flung out of the window by any man, but coaxed downstairs a step at a time." Until desired conduct becomes habitual, you can't call it faithfulness.

In the beginning, we develop habits by conscious attention to the little things, by being consistent, by step by step practice until the pattern of response is fixed and dependable. With the passing of time, taking care and keeping promises and fulfilling duties can become second nature to us. We not only seem, but we have become, faithful. The pattern is fixed.

On a recent morning I became self-conscious about my own pattern of preparing for the day. My routine seldom varies from the moment I leave the bed. There's a comfortable monotony to my ritual. No surprises. No thought required. Why this devotion to dullness? Because I'm only semi-conscious that early in the day. Lacking the brain-power to innovate, I function on automatic pilot. I've learned the hard way never to vary the system because if I do, later I'll not be able to remember whether I completed every vital step. For some reason Sundays are harder than other days. More than once I have had to drive back home before the first worship service because I couldn't remember whether I had applied deodorant, a critical oversight which would be evident to all by the time of the third service.

Some of my morning ablutions are performed for my sake, but as you can understand, several of them are performed for the sake of other people's good as well as my own. In little things like personal hygiene and in larger like fidelity to one's mate or sacrifice for one's country, the faithful person acts for the sake of the person, goal, or principle he loves, in spite of personal discomfort or danger such action may cause him. Faithfulness is love hanging on.

FAITHFULNESS IS LOVE BEING TRUSTWORTHY

Hanging on "in spite of" is what makes *faithfulness* worthy of trust. When a man says, "I love my wife" while sleeping with another woman, he is branded. He's an adulterer, a cheat, or a liar. We speak of his un-faithfulness. No matter how vehemently he protests, he cannot convince his skeptical accusers that he loves his wife. If he did, he would be faithful.

A man who protests, "I love my children" but can't be counted on to do his share in caring for them can hardly expect to be considered a loving and faithful father, can he?

How we discern whether a woman loves her job? We don't take her word for it. We observe instead such tell-tale evidence as the number of personal days she takes off, her record of tardiness, her promptness to leave at 5:00, her accumulated number of hours in voluntary overtime, her helpfulness toward her coworkers.

How, then, shall we measure one's love of the Lord? And of his church?

Where there is love, there is faithfulness.

I will declare that your love stands firm forever
and that you established your faithfulness in heaven itself (Ps 89:2).

The Psalmist's allusion to heaven, where God reigns and everything is in place, connotes trustworthiness. Looking heavenward, we see a dependable universe. Every day the sun rises and sets on schedule. Every day there is light and there is darkness. We can count on them, as on the progression of the seasons, the passing of the years. He who governs the earth from the heavens establishes the predictability of natural phenomena; they are evidence of the faithfulness of a loving God, the love of a faithful God.

Return to Psalm 89 for a moment.

> You [God] said, "I have made a covenant with
>   my chosen one,
>   I have sworn to David my servant,
> I will establish your line forever
>   and make your throne firm through all generations."
> The heavens praise your wonders, O Lord,
>   your *faithfulness* too, in the assembly of the holy
>   ones (3-5).

The Bible repeatedly (steadfastly, faithfully) presents the Lord as a covenant-making, covenant-keeping God. We seldom use the term *covenant* any more, but don't be thrown by it. It simply means God makes promises and keeps them. He is trustworthy.

Therefore we can take refuge in him:

> He who dwells in the shelter of the Most High will
>   rest in the shadow of the Almighty.
> I will say of the Lord, "He is my refuge and my fortress,
>   my God, in whom I trust" (Psalm 91:1).

> Surely he will save you from the fowler's snare and
>   from the deadly pestilence.
> He will cover you with his feathers,
>   and under his wings you will find refuge;
>   his *faithfulness* will be your shield and rampart (3, 4).

This is God as mother hen, sheltering her chicks with her

wings. Protecting, shielding, being faithful – such are the self-assigned duties of the God of love.

So far our focus has been on God, but we've been looking at his faithfulness to comprehend what ours must be. We've discovered an array of synonyms: to be faithful is to be loving, trustworthy, dependable, reliable. It is to be loyal, a trait I especially value. For many years I have been in leadership roles. Those years have taught me to appreciate loyalty (a synonym for faithfulness, remember) above almost any other trait.

I'm not alone. Harry Emerson Fosdick was of the opinion that

> any individual who ever achieved a rich, mature, satisfying personal life, did it only in so far as he was drawn together into coherence and significance by objective loyalties with which he identified himself.[3]

To what do we pledge allegiance, loyalty? In my experience, persons who pledge fealty to themselves are to be feared. They are faithful, certainly, but only to themselves. Everybody else is fair game. Watch out for the likes of them. On the other hand, the most secure, most fully developed, most honorable and most delightful persons I've known have given their allegiance to a cause bigger than themselves. Their loyalty elicits their trustworthiness and builds depth of character.

In one of his many books, Norman Vincent Peale relates an anecdote about Representative Martin Barnaby Madden of Illinois. Toward the end of his distinguished career, the elderly congressman was saddened to observe a young congressman vote whichever way certain power groups dictated. In addition, the young newcomer never openly dissented with anyone but always seemed in agreement with what was being said. Madden called his attention to what he was seeing. The congressman admitted the fault but didn't offer to amend it. "You know how it is, Mr. Madden. The external pressures on us legislators are tremendous."

"Young man," the senior congressman corrected, "I know all about the outer pressures. But where are your inner braces?"[4] Not a bad question, is it, for seekers of the fruit of the Spirit? Apparently the young congressman had not yet found a person or cause worthy his faithfulness, a failure that left him at the mercy of whoever pressed him for his vote.

Let me tell you about another young man, of whom I'm very proud. A leader in his church, attentive to his wife and a good example to his children, he had a well-deserved reputation as an exemplary Christian gentleman. His wide circle of acquaintances held him in high regard. They still do; they are unaware how close he came to smashing his reputation. You know about office romances. So did he. He never thought he might be vulnerable, though; he was unprepared for the overpowering pull of the young woman's attractiveness. He was reeling. Chemistry, we call it. He wanted her. She wanted him. And this upright, Christian man who had denounced others for cheating on their wives, suddenly understood. Predictably, he rationalized that somehow his case was different. Although even he couldn't believe his love-twisted logic, he still was tempted as never before in his life. He couldn't get her out of his mind. They just "happened" to meet in the hallway or on errands, found excuses to work late. You know the symptoms. The soap operas take their plots from real life.

This story has a happier ending than most. As I said, he really is an exemplary Christian gentleman. Aware of the danger he was in, he telephoned a friend, told him his story, and confessed, "I need help." The friends worked out a system for helping each other. In addition, he sought both psychological and spiritual counseling. The rather surpising conclusion to the story (one that would never make it to the soaps) is this. No affair developed, no homes were broken and no spouses were devastated. He succeeded in rebuffing the temptation, not because he didn't want to give in, not because she wasn't attractive, and not because his was a less than normal sex drive.

He overcame because he loved his wife and didn't want to hurt her, because he treasured the respect of his children, and because he was devoted to his church and feared what an affair would do to its reputation. Many years earlier he had pledged his allegiance to Christ; he could not bear to dishonor him now. He had some inner braces. Having long before decided to "live by the Spirit," he drew on the Spirit's inner strengthening when he needed it most.

One reason for my frequent fulminations against America's Look Out for Number One creed is that it not only wrecks havoc with community life but it also subjects its adherents to every temptation that comes along. You can always convince yourself that this or that deviation from morality is all right in your special case. Social laws were intended for other, less enlightened persons. You are above the law, more deserving than others, an exception. Fortunately, this Christian leader would not lie to himself. His loyalties brought him through.

He was, to put it simply, faithful. He passed Dr. Paul Tournier's test:

> Faithfulness without temptation to infidelity is not true faithfulness. Faith without temptation to doubt is not true faith. Purity without temptation to impurity is not true purity.[5]

It isn't the temptation that mars the record; it's the yielding.
FAITHFULNESS IS LOVE LIVING RIGHT

> Righteousness and justice are the foundation of your
> throne;
> love and faithfulness go before you (Ps 89:14).

Righteousness is right living; it is loving faithfulness in relationships. Justice is love generally applied, treating all persons
as loved ones are treated. Right living plus right loving equals
faithfulness.

We find this formula often in the Bible. Here is the 85th
Psalm:

> *Love* and *faithfulness* meet together; *righteousness* and
> *peace* kiss each other (10).

In this verse peace is introduced, the natural consequence of
love, faithfulness and righteousness in action.

Here is Proverbs 14:22:

> Do not those who plot evil go astray?
> But those who plan what is good find *love* and *faithfulness.*

This axiom mixes goodness and love and faithfulness, an olio
not unlike Paul's clustered fruit in Galatians 5:22 (love, joy,
peace, patience, kindness, goodness, faithfulness . . . .) Scripture summons us to Right Living – all the time. Not just every
once in a while, not just when the mood hits us. Faithfulness is
doing right by other people always, in all circumstances. It is
love living right even with those closest to us, who are not
always lovable.

Billy Graham likes to recount a lesson he learned as a youngster from Old Will, a hired hand on his father's farm. One evening they were talking together, Will and young Billy, under a mimosa tree, when the old man (who doubled as a lay preacher, with a theology that Graham said "often made up in color what it lacked in correctness") explained some of his thinking.

"Sanctification is a wonderful thing," he said. "The wonderful thing about it is that you can pick it up, and you can put it down."

He saw that Billy was puzzled, so he explained himself further. When he had come home for supper a few nights earlier, his wife called him a name that displeased him. Before he could stop himself, he had hit her over the head with a plate. You and I might have questioned his behavior in light of his Christian professions. No problem for him, though. He said the quarrel was "only an interlude in which he 'lain down' his sanctification temporarily."[6]

Old Will, sanctified before and sanctified afterward, pierced a parenthesis in his holiness long enough to clobber his wife. I doubt sanctification works that way, and I know faithfulness doesn't. It is love living right all the time.

FAITHFULNESS IS LOVE BEING PATIENT

But you, O Lord, are a compassionate and gracious God, slow to anger, abounding in *love* and *faithfulness* (Ps 86:15).

What Christian hasn't had need to claim this verse! Where would the believer be, without God's compassion and graciousness, love and faithfulness?

129

As a men's retreat in Oregon was closing, one of the campers asked to speak to me privately about a little problem. He was a fairly new Christian, grateful for the good things the Lord had done in his life. He'd suffered a heart attack, with the beneficial result that he was able to conquer his smoking habit. He appreciated the Lord's help in that victory, but was puzzled by his failure to correct another defect. The help he wanted from me had to do with his quick temper.

"What can I do to cure my anger?" he asked me. Inwardly I was smiling, because that's one question none of my friends would think of asking me. Before I could even try to offer any suggestions, I had to confess that the biggest struggle of my life has been my temper.

After my confession, we discussed the issue. I spoke to him a little bit about step-by-step character building and reminded him of Jesus' encouraging words, that he who is faithful in little will be faithful in much. "All I'm saying to you is that one's character is built up one step at a time. Don't give up on yourself. I haven't yet. And I do believe I'm seeing progress, though the struggle remains."

You may not understand our conversation. Please believe me, for some of us, particularly people with temperaments like his and mine, people who laugh quickly and cry quickly – and who are easily angered – there is hope. The Spirit does work with us, and his peace calms our fire.

As I'm writing these words I'm remembering an embarrassing moment on a Sunday in Innsbruck, Austria. Our tour group had made arrangements to use a room in the hotel for a communion service. It was a beautiful experience. One of our tour members, a minister, conducted the service, bringing a thoughtful meditation on the meaning of the Lord's sacrifice. As I was closing the service, I added a few comments about what he had to say and then I mentioned that for people in a tour group, being together for two weeks, living in close quarters with one another, is a microcosm of our learning peace on planet earth, requiring a great deal of tolerance, patience, grace and forgiveness.

It was, if I do say so, a good little speech. These elevating thoughts were uttered at about 9:30 AM. We left the hotel to do a walking tour of the old city of Innsbruck. Our German guide divided us into three groups. I was to lead one, Mike, my assistant, another, and she was to lead the third. There had been a little tension between our guide and me for a few days; things didn't always go to our mutual satisfaction, but on this Sunday morning I honestly didn't mean to misbehave. I was having trouble, however, holding my group together. Too many shops, too many diverse interests. Finally I gave up and released them to go their independent ways, setting 11:30 as the time for reconvening at the bus. That is what I thought the guide had earlier told us to do. I was wrong. She had told us 11:15.

When next I saw her, she unsmilingly asked me in a rather accusing tone, "Why did you tell your group to be back at 11:30 when I told them to be back at 11:15? Why?"

"I thought that's what you said." Well, she went on to explain (at some length and in considerable detail) exactly why she had said to be back at 11:15. The bus didn't have any place to park; it could only stop long enough to scoop us up and be off again. If there were a fifteen-minute delay, the driver would probably get a ticket, we'd be in all kinds of trouble and it would all be my fault.

I was sorry. I apologized. I groveled. It was my tour group

and I was really in charge, but I was penitent. Well, we walked on back to the bus where the driver was standing and people were boarding. I heard her say to him – she forgot to switch her English to German – "Some stupid idiot changed the time."

Remember those uplifting words I had spoken to our group just a few hours earlier about tolerance and patience and forgiveness? In that split second I forgot all of it. And everything I had stored up against her for three days came boiling out. A little later she and I held a peace conference, and I spent the remaining two days of the tour trying to make up to her for my outburst.

And the good man in Oregon asked me to help him control his temper!

Now you understand why I've been talking about the step-by-stepness of our growth in Christ. If you're built as I am – may the Lord have mercy on your soul – disappointing yourself is a much too frequent experience. It's especially troublesome when, after having preached to others, you practice the opposite. That's when it becomes so tempting to give up and hide behind a phalanx of excuses: "That's how I'm built; I can't help it; that's just me."

At such a moment we need to recall Paul's Galatian teaching on the fruit of the spirit. Calling them *fruit* emphasizes the truth that these virtues do not suddenly, spontaneously appear. They come to fruition gradually and are tested over time. The fruit is of the *Spirit*, a reminder that it's not "natural" for us always to be loving and joyful and peaceful and patient and kind and good and faithful. We have to have help, supernatural, Holy Spirit help.

Why didn't I give up and quit that day in Innsbruck? Because, though I embarrassed myself then – and am blushing again as I tell you about it – I believe I am getting better. You should have known me years ago. There has been progress, and I thank God for it. In addition, I know He isn't finished with me yet. In my early Christian Endeavor days I learned to say, "I can do all things through Christ who strengthens me." I believed it then. I believe it now.

Some leaders of our Indianapolis church and I used to play a little tennis. Not much tennis, you understand. I never became any good at it, but it was a source of relaxation and fellowship, and I loved it. The group played every week, providing comic relief for other members of the tennis club. As I said, I never became a good player, but now and then I would make a shot that was flawless. (That's when tennis players should quit and go home, but my partners wouldn't let me do that.) Every now and then I could come up with a brilliantly executed play, but no one ever called me a brilliant player; they never even called me a good player. An occasional respectable shot does not a good tennis player make. Watch some competent ones. The difference is too obvious. They are good routinely. Their excellence is predictable.

It's routine spiritual excellence that Galatians 5:22 and 23 describes, of a kind developed over a lifetime and kept in shape by regular exercise and practice. Susan Butcher, champion athlete in a sport you might not have even heard of, understands the principle well. She competes in the Iditarod, the gruelling thousand-mile dog sled race across Alaska. She's won the contest several years in a row. An interviewer asked her to account for her success. She said her chief competitor starts his dogs early and drives them hard; by the end of the day they are exhausted. Every day he forges ahead of her, but by sundown his dogs are running slower and she is catching up. She wins, she says, by not exploiting her dogs. She would lose a two or even one week race, but she wins in the longer contest.

Hers is good advice for running the race set before us Christians. The fruit of the Spirit is for the long haul. It won't help you get rich quick, nor outfox your competitors, nor catapult you to instant success. Instead, it enriches life exponentially, each year yielding a greater measure of love, joy, peace, patience, kindness, goodness, and faithfulness. Franz Kafka, not a Christian, nonetheless comes close to Christian truth in his opinion that "perhaps there is only one cardinal sin: impatience. Because of impatience we were driven out of Paradise; because of impatience we cannot return."[7]

Faithfulness is love being patient, and

"love always protects, always trusts, always

hopes, always perseveres. Love never fails" (1 Cor 13:7,8).

FOR YOUR FURTHER CONSIDERATION

1. How does a person develop the characteristic of faithfulness? What role does habit play?

2. What does this mean: "Faithfulness is love hanging on"? Hanging on to what? When?

3. The Bible repeatedly depicts the Lord as a covenant-making, covenant-keeping God. Why is it important to remember this fact when discussing faithfulness?

4. Congressman Martin Barnaby Madden spoke of "inner braces." What are they? Where can get some? Why do you need them?

5. How does faithfulness help you fight against temptation? What role does loyalty play in developing faithfulness? Where

does loyalty come from?

6. Can you explain why the elements mentioned in Psalm 85:10 belong together?

7. When it is spiritually acceptable to lay down your faithfulness?

8. What should you do when you fall away from your high Christian standards, either in a fit of temper or in a moment of forgetfulness?

9. This chapter defines faithfulness in part as "love being patient." Is that a definition you would give it? Can you offer another one?

Endnotes

1.Quoted in Bill Moyers, *A World of Ideas*, ed. Betty Sue Flowers. New York: Doubleday, 1989, p. 244.

2. Quoted in Os Guiness, *In Two Minds*. Downers Grove, IL: InterVarsity Press, p. 302.

3. Henry Emerson Fosdick, *On Being a Real Person*, p. 97.

4. Norman Vincent Peale, *A Guide to Self-Control*. Greenwich, CT: Fawcett Publications, 1965, p. 166.

5. Paul Tournier, *Guilt and Grace*. p. 45.

6. "Christ in the Believer," *The Word for This Century*. pp. 87, 88.

7. Quoted in W. H. Auden and Kronenberger, *The Viking Book of Aphorisms*. New York: Viking Press, 1962, p.83.

GENTLENESS ❧

1 Peter 3:15, 16

"The fruit of the Spirit is love, joy, peace, patience, kindness, goodness, faithfulness, *gentleness* . . . ."

My personal heroes, a miscellany of uncelebrated but singular characters, differ from one another in almost every way. Neither famous nor rich nor powerful, all of them have nevertheless touched my life and left me forever changed. Among them are a few former professors, some school and Sunday School teachers from a long time ago, members of current and former churches, work associates, the lady I live with and many more. Each has in one way or another elicited my admiration; all are unforgettable. A diverse and fascinating collection they are, yet they hold one thing in common. They all possess a gentleness of spirit.

They say opposites attract. Is it possible that they are my heroes because they have what I lack? Gentle people attract me, perhaps because theirs is a virtue I'm still seeking. I haven't despaired of attaining it, because what they have in such abundance is not out of reach of anyone, even someone as intense as I, who seeks the whole fruit of the Spirit.

1 Peter 3:15, 16 is an ideal place to begin our meditation.

> But in your heart set apart Christ as Lord. Always be prepared to give an answer to everyone who asks you to give the reason for the hope that you have. But do this with *gentleness* and respect, keeping a clear conscience, so that those who speak maliciously against your good behavior in Christ may be ashamed of their slander.

LET CHRIST BE YOUR LORD

If a disciple is to imitate his master, then Christ's follower will be gentle. We "set apart Christ as Lord," seeking most of all to please him who was gentlest of all. Children flocked to him, persons of no reputation or social standing were unafraid of him, and even women defied custom to be in his presence. There they were all safe.

Following Christ draws out our own gentleness, for we want to be like him, and like him we cease to push people aside to get what's coming to us. With his help we are taming our unruly selves. The ego is a terrible lord, fighting to be first, vying against any other self, viewing as enemy anyone who thwarts its will. The self must prevail. Almost every transaction becomes a contest of wills; no defeat is brooked. The ego cannot tolerate a challenge to its sovereignty; rudeness, perceived or real, must be dealt with. Gentleness does not characterize the egotist.

> But the fruit of the Spirit is love, joy, peace, patience, kindness, goodness, faithfulness, gentleness and self-control. Against such things there is no law (Gal 5:22, 23).

Obviously nobody needs protection against the Spirit-led personality. The self-server, on the other hand, can be dangerous:

> The acts of the sinful nature are obvious: sexual immorality, impurity and debauchery; idolatry and witchcraft; hatred, discord, jealousy, fits of rage, selfish ambition, dissensions, factions and envy (Gal 5:19f).

When the self is in charge, some kind of legislation must be enacted to shield the innocent. Pity whoever or whatever crosses the self on the chase.

Where God rules, the self cannot. A house divided against itself cannot stand; only God can be in charge of his kingdom, and where God is in charge, socially destructive behavior is forbidden. Thus, "I warn you, as I did before, that those who live like this will not inherit the kingdom of God," (Gal 5:21) where peaceful relationships prevail, and where the citizens are gentle men and women.

The merit, it must be emphasized, is gentleness, not weakness, a look-alike commonly mistaken for it, especially by your more machismo types. It helps to remember Moses – powerful Moses, forceful enough to lead an nation of stubborn, often rebellious, frequently ungrateful people to freedom – whom the Bible calls meekest man on earth. (Num 12:3, KJV). Not weakest, not wimpiest, but strong enough to be gentle, humble enough to obey.

In 2 Corinthians 10:1, the apostle Paul appeals for peace among some troubled and quarrelsome Christians with these surprising words:

> By the meekness and gentleness of Christ, I appeal to you –
> I, Paul, who am "timid" when face to face with you, but "bold" when away!

What kind of entreaty is this? Wouldn't you have expected him to refer to Christ's authority, or perhaps to his own as an apostle as he does elsewhere? No, in this troublesome situation he alludes to the Christ who did not chose to escape a cross by sneaking out of Gethsemane by a back way, who wouldn't allow his disciples to do battle with his captors, who stoically endured the mockery of a rigged trial, and who did not try to save himself, he who had rescued so many others. No one can read the Gospels and conclude he was weak. He was, to the contrary, strong enough not to fight back, sure enough to submit to the injustice, trusting his Father sufficiently to deal gently even with his assassins.

Such muscular gentleness deserves further meditation, doesn't it? One of my unforgettable lessons comes from my teen years. I have undoubtedly recounted my education in gentleness elsewhere in my writings, but I can't mention the subject without recalling three separate but related lessons. The first came in an advertisement for Scotch Tape. (I mentioned this in a sermon once. It was discouraging to learn how many people in the congregation couldn't remember ever having seen it. They were too young, they said. How can they, they who look almost elderly, be so much younger than I?) Surely you, dear reader, recall that square-jawed, unshaven, muscular guy wearing a striped T-shirt who held up the Scotch Tape dispenser and uttered the slogan, "Tough but oh, so gentle." A friend of mine insists the ad was for Scott Tissue and not Scotch Tape. Memory fails one sometimes. I wonder which one of us is wrong.

Tough . . . gentle. Not words commonly associating with one another.

I paid attention to it because about the same time the ad was appearing Mrs. Near, my piano teacher, was attempting to teach the relationship between tough (or strong) and gentle. She had assigned Debussy's "Clair de Lune." If you are familiar with this beautiful piece, you know a section in it calls for triple pianissimo, to be played very, very softly. Soft wasn't my style, so I banged through it with my usual animated fortissimo, to her pained displeasure. Patient and kind though she was, she couldn't tolerate any more. She had to change my style. With exquisite tact, she converted me.

"Roy," she said gently, "you have strong hands." You probably can't fully appreciate how much it meant to the undersized little boy I was to be told I had strong anything! "Do you know that it takes a lot more strength to play softly than to play loudly?" I promise you, "Clair de Lune" was never rendered more gently. I wanted to prove how strong I was.

Apparently the lesson wasn't transferred to other areas of my life, though, because I remember yet another lesson. It was just a little moment, one my Dad probably quickly forgot, but one I never did. While reading a magazine he came across an article on social tact. Then he applied it. He left the magazine open to that page and later said, as if by the way, that there was an article I might enjoy reading. When I picked it up, I knew exactly what he was trying to tell me. Apparently I hadn't dealt very "softly" with some people. No one ever accused Dad of being weak, but they honored him as a gentle-man. He wanted the same for his son.

Gentleness is not a virtue everyone admires. George Bush, in fact, felt it necessary when campaigning for the presidency, to prove to his countrymen that he was tough. Journalists had raised the issue of "the wimp factor," worrying the soft-spoken candidate might not be man enough for the job. The wild-west ethic rides on. Gentleness is not high on the list of attributes American males aspire to display.

Given America's social mores, men especially come to the Scriptures unprepared for these injunctions to be gentle. Yet it is apparent that this is an attribute of the disciple of Jesus. For example, here's Philippians 4:5:

Let your gentleness be evident to all. The Lord is near.

In these brief sentences Paul exhorts and then explains. "The Lord is near" yields two meanings: If Christ's return is imminent, we don't have to resort to fighting because the Ultimate Arbitrator will soon straighten everything out. That's one possibility. The other: "The Lord is near (at hand)." He is with us, present in his Spirit, his might available for our use. We don't have to prove any physical or psychological or political prowess; we can rest in his power and sovereignty. Being indwelt by his Spirit, we are so strong we can afford to be gentle.

The Spirit's gentleness is hard to bring to maturity in the individualistic soil of our culture. Alexis DeToqueville made this discovery early in the nineteenth century. The keen-eyed Frenchman visited America ostensibly to study our penal system, but while was at it he observed and commented on American life and customs. After returning to to France he wrote his travel memoirs in a book which Americans have carefully studied ever since. In it he warns against this threat to social stability called "individualism." He was right. This toxic doctrine justifies my putting selfish interests first, ahead of community, church, nation, family, friends – anybody. If everybody subscribes to this most popular of "isms," the nation loses coherence and descends rapidly into anarchy. You can see it happening.

The antidote for this poison is to let somebody else be lord. That somebody is Christ. For where many are worshiping, obeying, submitting to the same Lord, there is harmony.

BE PREPARED TO EXPLAIN YOUR HOPE

1 Peter doesn't present the ability "to explain the hope that is in you" as a source of the strength of gentleness, but it is. When we know what we know and know how we know it, we aren't compelled to be incessantly trying to prove something. I am still embarrassed when I recall my Bible college years; with my smattering of biblical knowledge I was ready to take on anybody, anywhere in religious debate. My purpose was to defeat my opponents no matter how I had to do it. What made me so scrappy? Uncertainty. Like sophomores ("wise fools") everywhere, I had to prove my stuff.

Peter says:

Always be prepared to give an answer to everyone who asks you to give the reason for the hope that you have.

Be prepared to give an answer, he says. In immature eagerness to do battle, I'd offer the answer before anyone asked the question. Peter certainly is not fomenting religious war here, yet this verse has too often been ripped from its context to justify verbal pugilistics. Not attacking, but answering, is his counsel. Then he tells how to do it – gently ("Do this with gentleness and respect"). He urges us to be knowledgeably secure enough to focus on hope, not on insecurities or doctrines. Gentleness is rooted in confidence, as feistiness is in insecurity. Our hope is in the Lord, knowledge of whom makes it possible for us to ease into gentleness.

> Who is going to harm you if you are eager to do good? But even if you should suffer for what is right, you are blessed. Do not fear what they fear; do not be frightened (13, 14).

The person who knows who he is, whose he is, where he's going and that he's certain of getting there can deal gently even when he is not gently dealt with in return.

Someone has astutely observed that if American drivers (in their cars) were lined up, all hundreds of thousands of them bumper to bumper, 93 per cent of them would pull out to pass. They'd all want to get there first. In flying I'm often amused at passengers pushing and shoving and elbowing and toe-stomping to board the plane first. They must get ahead of everybody else, even though the plane isn't going anywhere until everyone is safely seated. In their anxiety to look out for themselves, they perceive their fellow travelers as the enemy, or at least the competition.

It is not so among seasoned travelers. They're relaxing in the lounge reading the paper, watching the crowd go by, and when the rest of the passengers are aboard, they amble in. They know who they are and where they're going and are certain of getting there; the plane is not going to leave without them.

They are at ease.

One of the most popular ministers among my acquaintances is often a subject of conversation when some of his many friends are together. They love to tell the one about a funeral service he and another minister conducted. Afterward, the two men rode together in his car to the cemetery, following the hearse in the procession. My friend was driving and chatting amicably with his colleague. Somewhere along the route, for a moment forgot what he was doing. He suddenly became very impatient with that slow vehicle in front of him, tooted his horn, pulled out and passed. When his eyes caught the startled look on the funeral director's face, he realized what he had done and sort of slithered his sedan back in line.

It could happen to anybody. His embarrassing tale is retold to point out what occurred when he forgot who he was and where he was going. The formerly relaxed, kindly minister became another aggressive motorist. He lost his gentleness.

"But life is difficult," someone will protest. He tells the truth.

"In Christ we can overcome the difficulty," we answer. We tell a stronger truth.

BE GENTLE AND RESPECTFUL

But do this with gentleness and respect (verse 16).

They are inseparable, aren't they? Gentleness and respect. We treat sympathetically those we respect. This can best be appreciated by observing the antithesis. Paul offers it in 1 Timothy 6:10f. His subject is money, or more specifically, that perverted love of it which so brutalizes human relationships.

> For the love of money is a root of all kinds of evil. Some people, eager for money, have wandered from the faith and pierced themselves with many griefs. But you, man of God, flee from all this, and pursue righteousness, godliness, faith, love, endurance and gentleness.

You know people, too many of them, hot in pursuit of a deal, a bargain, a buck. You know them and retreat from their path. Theirs is not the way of gentleness.

"Flee from all this," Paul urges. Concern yourself with persons. They are more deserving of your respect.

The desire to be respected is universal; individuals and nations go to incredible lengths to get it. In the tense years leading up to America's secession from England, for example, Sir Joseph Yorke, bemoaning Britain's inability to repress rebellion in the colonies, urged Lord Suffolk, a minister in Lord North's government, "to restore the appearance which Britain had such a right to assume," thus insuring that her neighbors would again speak the "language of respect and friendship."[1] Respect is what Kaiser's Germany wanted in 1914; what Hitler's fought for in 1938-45. The hunger for respect seems to be the reason for America's foreign policies, even though the proper political term is "national interest."

The politically incorrect but very wise Golden Rule is actually the only sure guide to peaceful international relations. If nations would do unto others as they would have others do unto them, the peace this world yearns for would follow. How much greater would be the peace among persons if, respecting one another, they would not think too highly of themselves and too disparagingly of others.

> We have the nicest garbage man,
> He empties out our garbage can;

He's just as nice as he can be,
He always stops and talks to me.
My mother doesn't like his smell,
But then, she doesn't know him well.[2]

She judges him, you see, by his odor. She has more respect for her social discernment than for his service. He's not one of her kind.

On a tour to the Holy Land we visited Israel's gruesome memorial to the Holocaust. The Israelis don't want the world to forget what happened to Europe's Jews. In ghastly detail the museum retold the story of the Nazis' inhuman extermination of six million men, women and children. What has largely been forgotten is the fact that the death camps were originally designed for a different purpose. Ayrans, and not Jews, were targeted for destruction there. The master race had to be perfected. Therefore all crippled, deformed, elderly, insane, and unproductive persons were considered fuel for the ovens' fires. The judges between the living and soon dead were Germany's doctors, professionals who had sworn to protect and preserve human lives. Under Hitler they cast aside their oaths and became state executioners. Their discarded oath said in part, "I will maintain the utmost respect for human life from the time of conception, even under threat."[3] But they forgot. They would not preserve whom they did not respect.

Where respect is absent, expect no gentleness.

KEEP A CLEAR CONSCIENCE, ABOVE CRITICISM

But do this with gentleness and respect, keeping a clear conscience, so that those who speak maliciously against your good behavior in Christ may be ashamed of their slander.

At first blush the relationship of a clear conscience to a gentle demeanor may not be apparent. In the verse quoted above, Peter doesn't make the connection; the reason for "keeping a clear conscience," he says, is to counter any slander. The phrase immediately follows "with gentleness and respect," though, hinting an affinity between the phrases similar to our familiar saying, "A good offense is the best defense." In matters of conscience, someone with something to hide characteristically charges someone else with it. A bad conscience makes a good critic. When someone tells you, for example, "I don't go to church; there are too many hypocrites there," you haven't learned a thing about the church but you have learned that the critic is well acquainted with hypocrisy. We all find our sins in others, and we don't deal with them gently.

Some time ago Kurt Waldheim, president of Austria, was barraged by criticism from other nations, including especially the United States. Charged with being a Nazi officer during World War II, Waldheim protested his innocence, but his words were not believed. I don't know whether he told the truth or not, but one statement he made caused me to doubt him. "Who does not make mistakes?" he pleaded, then added, "But I have not really done anything wrong." Then he is, after Jesus, the only person who hasn't. Such protestations of innocence never fail to alarm me.

On this subject, the Bible cannot be argued down. The evidence is overwhelming: "All have sinned and fall short of the glory of God" (Rom 3:23). Who dares say, "I have done nothing wrong"?

Of course, I am taking two sentences and wrenching them out of context, which is unfair to the Austrian president. My reaction is not to his specific situation, but to his all-too-human denial of wrong-doing. A friend of mine who spent some time in prison probably exaggerated when he said all the inmates were innocent, to hear them tell it, but most of them at least tried to convince anyone who would listen that they were jailed in error.

When Waldheim protested his innocence, I wished I could do the same. In fact, if I could change the language of the Bible here, I would. Where it says, "But do this with gentleness and respect, keeping a clear conscience," I wish it read " . . . keeping a *cleared* conscience." Then I could comply.

Actually, this is the import of verse 18 and following:

> For Christ died for sins once for all, the righteous for the unrighteous [that includes you and me], to bring you to God. He was put to death in the body but made alive by the Spirit, through whom also he went and preached to the spirits in prison who disobeyed long ago when God waited patiently in the days of Noah while the ark was being built. In it only a few people, eight in all, [Noah, his wife and their three sons and their wives] were saved through water, and this water symbolizes baptism that now saves you, not the removal of dirt from the body but the pledge of a good conscience toward God.

It isn't that we have a clear conscience. We are conscious of our sins. We can't protest our innocence but we can attest, "I appealed to God, who heard my appeal and through my submitting to him in faith and repentance and baptism, cleared my conscience. He treats me as innocent and now I'm free."

This liberation from a guilty conscience also tears away our defenses. We have nothing to cover up, nothing to explain, nothing to defend, and therefore no need to accuse. We can live transparently and congenially. We don't have to put others down to build ourselves up. Not oblivious to their shortcomings, we feel nonetheless feel no compulsion to criticize, because we aren't oblivious to our own. We know we're no better than they are, but we also know that we're no worse. Before the Lord, we are equal. Only his grace makes the difference.

You'll remember my cautioning you that sometimes this study might not seem to be about spiritual life, since so little is said about the standard criteria of spirituality, which I treat in other books. This would be rather a study of Christian character, to demonstrate that spirituality cannot be separated from morality, which has to do with acceptable social conduct. Right treatment of others ("righteousness") is what the Lord expects of his disciples. He calls it loving one another.

Dr. Carl Jung, a famous psychoanalyst, was once visited by a brilliant young man seeking psychoanalysis. Indeed, he had already analyzed himself. He presented Dr. Jung with a written detailed analysis of his findings. After reading it, the analyst told the man he was correct on every point. Then Jung asked himself why the young man wasn't cured. He was intellectually correct; what was wrong, he found, was his bad attitude. Jung learned that he had been befriended by an older school teacher who sacrificed to help him fulfill his potential.

He returned her kindness with self-indulgence. He accepted her money, enjoyed wonderful winter vacations and satisfied his every whim at her expense, with no qualms of conscience. Dr. Jung concluded, "His fundamental error lay in his moral attitude. The man wouldn't admit any connection between his morality and his sickness, or between science and morality." After all, he said, the lady had given of her free will. That should clear him. "But instead," Jung said, "at a lower and a deeper level, he was a sick man." To Jung, "The moral attitude is a real factor in life with which the psychologist must reckon if he is not to commit the gravest errors."[4]

A prominent contemporary psychiatrist, Dr. Thomas Szasz, created a stir among his colleges by insisting there is no such thing as mental illness, but what we have been labeling mental illnesses are really moral problems. His fellow psychiatrists have mostly written him off as a pesky gadfly, but they may have been too hasty. There's some truth in his charge. So-called "mental illness" manifests itself in asocial behavior. Psychologically healthy persons enjoy good social relationships because they treat others with respect and gentleness. For this reason biblical teachers call believers to a morality that includes loving God as essential, but incomplete in itself. Equally essential to one's spiritual life is loving people and treating them right. It's a difficult requirement, impossible of achievement on our own strength. Interpersonal relationships are demanding, exhausting, requiring a spirit of gentle patience and inextinguishable love. The Spirit makes such a spirit possible.

In this chapter, then, *morality*, *spiritual life*, *character* and *psychological health* have been treated as virtual synonyms to underscore the biblical truth that spirituality cannot be separated from social intercourse. To love God is insufficient; God's Word calls for more:

> For anyone who does not love his brother, whom he has seen, cannot love God, whom he has not seen. And he has given us this command: Whoever loves God must also love his brother (1 John 4:20, 21).

> Love the Lord your God with all your heart and with all your soul and with all your mind . . . .Love your neighbor as yourself (Matt 22:37, 39).

> Be completely humble and *gentle*; be patient, bearing with one another in *love*. Make every effort to keep the unity of the

Spirit through the bond of peace (Eph 4:2, 3).

The Spirit is bringing his fruit to maturity in the disciples of Christ; he enables the spiritually sensitive person to act gently in love. When he is allowed to be in charge, the Spirit-filled individual cultivates a fruitful life.

And the fruit of the Spirit is

Love

  Joy

    Peace

      Patience

        Kindness

          Goodness

            Faithfulness

              Gentleness.

FOR YOUR FURTHER CONSIDERATION

1. "Ladies and gentlemen," the master of ceremonies intones. What does he mean? To whom is he speaking?

2. What is the difference among gentleness, meekness, weakness, and being "wimpy"?

3. In what way or ways does our belief that the Lord is at hand help us to be gentle?

4. Do you agree that gentleness and respect belong together? Always? What kind of respect? For whom?

5. The author writes, "In matters of conscience, someone with something to hide characteristically charges someone else with it." Have you noticed this phenomenon? What does it have to do with the relationship between a clear conscience and a gentle spirit?

6. Why does the Christian speak of a *cleared* rather than a *clear* conscience?

7. By this late stage in your reading of the book, do you agree or disagree with author's premise that "spirituality cannot be separated from morality"?

Endnotes

1. Barbara W. Tuchman, *The First Salute*. New York: Alfred A. Knopf, 1988, p. 75.

2. Catherine Marshall, *Mr. Jones, Meet the Master – Sermons and Prayers of Peter Marshall*. New York: Fleming H. Revell Co.,. 1949, 1950, p. 59.

3. Paul Meier and Linda Burnett, *The Unwanted Generation*. Grand Rapids: Baker Book House, 1980, p. 117.

4. C. G. Jung, *Modern Man in Search of a Soul*. New York: Harcourt, Brace and World, Inc., A Harvest Book, 1933, p. 192.

SELF-CONTROL ❧

Romans 6:19-23

"And the fruit of the Spirit is love, joy, peace, patience, kind-ness, goodness, faithfulness, gentleness, *self-control.*"

The final virtue is Paul's list is a magnificent achievement. To appreciate it fully, read carefully the following selection from Romans 6, noting every occurrence of the accented word.

> What then? Shall we sin because we are not under law but under grace? By no means! Don't you know that when you offer yourselves to someone to obey him as *slaves*, you are *slaves* to the one whom you obey – whether you are *slaves* to sin, which leads to death, or to obedience, which leads to righteousness? But thanks be to God that, though you used to be *slaves* to sin, you wholeheartedly obeyed the form of teaching

to which you were entrusted. You have been set free from sin and have become slaves to righteousness.

I put this in human terms because you are weak in your natural selves. Just as you used to offer the parts of your body in *slavery* to impurity and to ever increasing wickedness, so now offer them in *slavery* to righteousness leading to holiness. When you were *slaves* to sin, you were free from the control of righteousness. What benefit did you reap at that time from the things you are now ashamed of? Those things result in death. But now that you have been set free from sin and have become *slaves* to God, the benefit you reap leads to holiness, and the result is eternal life. For the wages of sin is death, but the gift of God is eternal life in Christ Jesus our Lord (15-23).

The term *self-control* in Galatians 5 is a little misleading. It sounds as if we are capable of controlling ourselves, which is not what Paul has been teaching in the chapter. *Self-control* actually signifies a self that is controlled, but not by the self.

The Greek word is *enkrateia*, translated as self-control in the New International Version but as *temperance* in the King James. Common usage has narrowed the latter's application to moderation in consumption of alcoholic beverages. Too bad, since otherwise the King James would be preferable to the more modern translation. Paul really has in mind a temperate character, one not given to outbursts of excess or unharnessed exuberance. The will is not self-controlled so much as Spirit-controlled. Self-control, as Paul uses the word, is personal will power under the dominion of the Spirit of God, authority over oneself empowered by the stronger might of the Holy Spirit.

In 1 Corinthians 9 Paul employs the same Greek word (*enkrateia*) as an athletic metaphor, thinking this time in strictly human terms.

Everyone who competes in the prizes goes into strict training. (*Strict training* is NIV for *enkrateia*.)

Here's the same sentence in the King James Version:

Every man that striveth for the mastery is temperate in all things. (In this case, *temperate* translates *enkrateia*.)

The athlete disciplines himself, his will to win dominating his body. In this verse, *strict training* seems the better translation. Athletic contests don't call for moderation but strict, disciplined, sometimes agonizing work.

Disciplined will power subjects the body to profitable punishment. But what can train the will? Is *self*-will sufficient? Whoever has really tried to corral a wild will knows the answer. Since his Corinthian readers were as enamored of athletic contests as contemporary Americans are, Paul borrows an analogy from Greek sports. He raises the stakes, though, when he adds, "They do it to get a crown that will not last; but we do it to get a crown that will last forever." By *we* he means disciples of Jesus, who train for a prize not awarded on any earth-bound playing field, who are after an eternal, spiritual reward. Our contest requires more than Greek self-mastery. To gain the prize we're after requires God-mastery of the self.

How is it to be achieved?

ACKNOWLEDGE WHO
IS IN CHARGE OF YOUR LIFE

Scriptures present diametrically opposed forces at work in the world: the power of God and the lesser but still effective power of Satan. According to John, Satan pretty much has his way for the time being:

We know that we are children of God and that the whole world is under the control of the evil one (5:19).

We've experienced enough of his mischief to perceive he's up to no good. We regularly contrast his domain with God's by our use of *worldliness* for Satan's realm and *godliness* for God's. Where do we live? In the middle, pressured from both directions but frequently leaning Satanward ("going to the devil," we call it) because he makes the way so much easier than God does. An uncontrolled will just naturally drifts down the path of least resistance. When Paul names self-control in his fruit-of-the-Spirit cluster, he means a will fighting against the current, moving upstream by a power greater than the downward pull of Satan.

Note: I have mentioned the authority of God or the evil one. Nothing has been mentioned of freedom from authority. That's not an alternative. In reading the Romans passage that opened this chapter, you paid close attention to the word *slave* and its cognate, *slavery*. Did you grasp the spiritual principle Paul takes for granted in those verses? He distinguishes two different forms of slavery. You might have expected him to set up a polarity between freedom and slavery to sin. He doesn't. The opposites are slavery to sin and freedom from sin, all right, but freedom from sin is achieved through another kind of slavery, to God. Total human autonomy is not mentioned – because it is not possible. Our egos are not designed for absolute sovereignty. God reserved that privilege for himself. We come closest to genuine freedom when we most closely identify our wills with his. The greater the extent of his lordship in our lives, the lesser is Satan's sway over us. We can take comfort in Paul's confession in Romans 7. His is the desperate state of a person yearning but unable to do right; his will power can't overcome his natural affinity for sin:

158

We know that the law is spiritual; but I am unspiritual, sold as a slave to sin. I do not understand what I do. For what I want to do I do not do, but what I hate I do. And if I do what I do not want to do, I agree that the law is good. As it is, it is no longer I myself who do it, but it is sin living in me (14-17).

Something alien to my better self has taken over, "for though I have the desire to do good, I can't carry it out." (Does this sound familiar?)

For what I do is not the good I want to do; no, the evil I don't want to do – this I keep on doing. Now if I do what I do not want to do, it is no longer I who do it, but it is sin living in me that does it (18-20).

The struggle accelerates, the vacillations madden. He is helplessness to stop them. Finally he cries out,

What a wretched man I am! Who will rescue me from the body of death?

The answer is not so much a reply as a doxology.

Thanks be to God – through Jesus Christ our Lord!

Here is hope. Rescue comes from God, who pays for our release from slavery through Christ's redemptive work on the cross. Thanks to him, we are no longer in bondage to sin.

But God didn't purchase our freedom only to set us adrift again. Drift's direction is always downward. Our freedom is not absolute, but conditional. He is now in charge. We have not been given self-mastery but God-mastery. If he had granted total liberty, before long we'd be right back where we were. Ask any reformed alcoholic how free he is to drink again. By God's grace we have been liberated from the evil one – and from ourselves. Our prospects are infinitely better than they were because our new master is infinitely better than our old

159

one.

If you found the last few paragraphs a bit too "theological," let's approach the subject from a different angle. A popular topic for discussion today is the addictive society. Ministers don't need to be informed of the dramatic increase in incidences of compulsive-obsessive behavior. At the beginning of my ministry, an addict was either an alcoholic or a drug abuser. Today the category has broadened to include a host of persons hooked on nicotine, sex, food, power, work, violence, thrills, and many other almost unimaginable compulsions.

Addictive-compulsive behavior is more prominent than ever before, I suspect, because Americans have believed the lie that freedom to do whatever we want to is a constitutional right. An entire nation boasting of personal freedom has enslaved itself to its appetites.

That's what happens when you think you can have it all. Surely, you reason, there is a third alternative between God's way and Satan's way. Let's be reasonable. We can work out some compromise here. It's the American way.

Compromise, the art of politics, is the fatal disease of character. Tip O'Neill, a master of compromise during his longtime tenure as Speaker of the House of Representatives, recounts a delightful story of his education in the art. His baseball loving father was watching a group of kids play a Sunday afternoon game. The batter hit a line drive over second base, a good easy single which he tried to stretch into a double. The umpire called him out at second. Immediately all his teammates jumped off the bench, yelling their protests. The ump changed his mind and called him safe.

Then an antiphonal roar of protests erupted from the other team.

The rhubarb lasted for ten minutes, until the umpire returned the batter to first base, the other players resumed their positions, and the game proceeded.

Mr. O'Neill had never seen anything like it, so after the game he walked over to the umpire and asked for an explanation.

He got one. The ump said when he realized they weren't getting anywhere, he asked how many thought the runner was safe. Nine hands went up. Then he asked how many thought he was out. The other nine went up. Then he asked, "How many of you say he was safe when he rounded first base?" All eighteen players raised their hands, so I sent him back to first.[1]

Mr. O'Neill said that's what compromise is, "finding areas where both sides can agree."

Compromise is often helpful although I still wonder about that ump's call. In politics, it's essential. But in matters moral and spiritual, compromise is disastrous. You can't bargain with vice and retain your virtue. You'll serve one master or the other. There is no third.

I may have misled your thinking a bit. I used the word *compromise*, which is not the term of preference today. We more readily speak of *tolerance*, by which we usually mean the state of having no convictions on the matter. We Americans pride ourselves on our tolerant society. We live and let live. We keep an open mind. We would be wiser, however, to align ourselves with the person who warned, "Keep an open mind; an open mind can be a very good thing, but don't keep your mind so open your brains fall out."[2] In recent years there has been a decided disappearance of brain-power among America's moralists.

Paradoxically, the way of the moral compromiser appears

far easier than the way of one sold out either to God or to Satan, but appearance is not reality. As Richard Halverson has rightly observed,

> It's always the fence-rider whose life is in precarious balance, who walks like a man on a tight rope . . . .He is like a man riding two horses that are running off in opposite directions. The strain is terrible.[3]

Relief from the strain comes in making the choice to ride just one horse, to obey one master. Who will be in charge of your life? We're back to the only two viable possibilities: either God, or his arch-rival. You aren't an option.

GO FOR THE BEST BENEFITS YOU CAN GET

Here's another question only you can decide. Which set of benefits do you want, those offered by God or by sin?

> What benefit did you reap at that time [before you became Christians] from the things you are now ashamed of? Those things result in death." But now that you have been set free from sin and have become slaves to God, the benefit you reap leads to holiness, and the result is eternal life (Romans 6:21, 22).

There you have it: serve sin and die, or serve God and become holy and live forever. Hardly seems a difficult choice, does it? No, not now, as you quietly read this book. Right now you know exactly which option you prefer. But out there, in the real world with its promises of spectacular profits and the good life – well, the alternative looks pretty inviting, too.

A few years ago good friends Larry and Eileen Carr sent a birthday card that shows how this works. On the front it says,

> "I didn't know what to get you for your birthday so I asked

the Great Weevil. He said a sports car. Then I asked the Little Weevil and he said a birthday card." [On the inside the card says]: "Naturally I chose the "lesser of the two Weevils."[4]

Greater and lesser Weevils make good greeting cards but lousy counselors. The Bible simply doesn't recognize gradations of evil. One Master leads to good and life, and the other to sin and death – often counterfeited as "the good life."

Beware of counterfeits. Be advised against pretending a commitment that you don't have. If we say we are serving God, then we must be certain we are serving God, not merely using him to attain something else we value more highly. God won't suffer being reduced to the status of a personal valet.

Counterfeit conversion is on my mind because of an article in our local newspaper about Mickey Davis, owner of a West Virginia striptease joint. A year earlier he "got religion" and shut down his place, reopening it as a revival center. At first the crowds came and Davis was thriving on his celebrity-convert status. The 700 Club of Christian Broadcasting Network did a feature on the club's conversion from skin to Spirit. Davis' high lasted a couple months. Then the crowds fell off, the money dried up, and the convert reconverted. Since Christians were not patronizing the revival center, he reopened the Fantasy Girls club as The Pink Pussycat and featured exotic entertainment and total nude revues.

When he shut down the first time, Davis announced he had had everything, including money, drugs, and women, and they left him feeling empty inside. So he tried religion. When his revival center failed, he castigated Christians for being phony and for not supporting his effort. "If people worshiped God like they do their money, this would have worked," he said.[5]

Had Davis really chosen God? Or had he chosen for God to provide his income? Was his fundamental value God or money?

BENEFIT OF SLAVERY TO SIN

"For the wages of sin is death."

You may not like what you're about to read. My opinion regarding the AIDS scare is a minority view. You won't see and hear it on network television broadcasts. They'll tune in on street demonstrations on behalf of more tax money for AIDS research and care for AIDS victims, but they won't seriously present this less popular side of the issue. How I wish, though, that somebody somewhere in high office would have the courage to admit there is a moral dimension to the AIDS issue. Won't anyone up there say, "One way not to get AIDS is to practice biblical sexual morality"? With certain rare exceptions (as in transfusing tainted blood or contracting the disease from medical workers), AIDS is the simplest of diseases to avoid. Nobody forces you to take drugs. Nobody forces you to sleep around. Rape is a possibility, of course, but fortunately that's the exception to the norm. Almost nobody's presenting this viewpoint. Of course not. Who wants to hear some prophet pronounce, "The wages of sin is death"?

Is abstinence totally unacceptable? "It must be dreadful," a man writes to *Time's* editor, "to have to postpone sex until after the fifth or sixth date. If this continues, people may end up having meaningful relationships." Is he so beside the point nobody will hear? Paul is concerned about much, much more than sexual behavior, of course. He hurts for the victims of every kind of slavery – except slavery to God and his righteousness.

Give in. Go along. Compromise. How can it hurt?

It can hurt terribly. I've never met an addict who ever intended to become one. Each one just gave in a little, experimented, went along, compromised. No thought was given that in so doing, there would be dire "benefits."

Jesus' treatment of subject is radical. Here, for instance, he prescribes a way to resist temptation to adultery:

> If your right eye causes you to sin, snatch it out and throw it away, for it is better for you to lose one part of your body than for your whole body to be thrown into hell. If your right hand causes you to sin, cut it off and throw it away (Matt 5:29, 30).

Why such drastic measures to protect against such a popular sin? Because the "benefits" are so grievous, that's why. Who deliberately opts for death?

BENEFIT OF SLAVERY TO GOD

"Holiness" is Paul's word. It is defined as "being set apart as special to God." Eternal life is what it leads to. Elsewhere Paul describes the difference in benefits this way:

> Join with others in following my example, brothers, and take note of those who live according to the pattern we gave you. For, as I have often told you before and now say again even with tears, many live as enemies of the cross of Christ. Their destiny [having chosen not to serve the Lord] is destruction, their god is their stomach, and their glory is in their shame. Their mind is on earthly things. But *our citizenship is in heaven.* And we eagerly await a Savior from there, the Lord Jesus Christ, who, by the power that enables him to bring everything under his control, *will transform our lowly bodies so that they will be like his glorious body.* Therefore, my brothers, you whom I love and long for, my joy and crown, that is how you should stand firm in the Lord, dear friends! (Phil 3:17-4:1).

I'll give you another example of holy behavior. In the English chapel at Stanton Herald these words are inscribed:

In the Year 1653
When all things sacred were
Throughout the Nation
Either Demolished or Profaned
Sir Robert Shirley Baronet
Founded this Church
Whose singular Praise it is
To have done the Best Things
in the Worst Times (And)
Hoped them in the Most Calamitous[6]

Sir Robert apparently did not compromise, even under the worst of circumstances. He had made his choice.

We can adopt basically one of three stances toward the world:

"Let us seek the world and enjoy it," says the pagan.

"We must flee the world and hide from it," says the hermit.

"Let us love the world and change it," says the disciple. To choose discipleship requires that we first change ourselves. To do so we give ourselves to the Creator of the world and let him who made all things good re-make us good so we can be good for, and good in, the world.

TAKE CONTROL BY GIVING UP CONTROL

You are undoubtedly familiar with the Twelve-Step program of Alcoholics Anonymous. Hundreds of thousands of alcoholics and other substance abusers have found sobriety and serenity through this simple but effective discipline. It's a program which could be of benefit to everyone. Of particular importance is the first step, which acknowledges the need of a higher power to overcome addiction.

AA says we need help. Yet Robert Schuller, that popular purveyor of possibility thinking, often sounds as if self-help is sufficient. Somewhere he warns against following the advice, "Take care," since by taking care people never get anywhere. To manage problems requires that persons "take control" rather than take care, he insists. A popular proverb also implies we can manage on our own:

A fool gives full vent to his anger, but a wise man keeps himself under control (Prov 29:11).

1 Thessalonians 4:4, in a paragraph dealing with sexual immorality, also sounds as if taking charge is within our own power:

Each of you should learn to control his own body in a way that is holy and honorable.

Who is right, AA or Schuller and Scripture?

Paul's advice to the Thessalonians is contained in a paragraph that begins, "It is God's will that you should be sanctified: that you should avoid sexual immorality . . . " and warns that the Lord "will punish men for all such sins." Again, he seems to be calling for a self-discipline that has but to be called upon to be effective. Keep reading. The good news comes in verse eight, as the paragraph closes:

Therefore, he who rejects this instruction does not reject man but God, *who gives you his Holy Spirit.*

All along Paul has been assuming a higher power. Here he identifies him as the Holy Spirit, the disciple's companion and enabler.

Dr. Leslie Weatherhead published the following letter, written by a friend of his during a Japanese bombing raid. It is one man's testimony to the unseen Source of strength.

> I didn't want to be killed . . . But I knew that if I were killed it would be absolutely all right, not because there would be nothingness, but because there would be goodness and richer experience beyond the grave . . . I felt as though some unseen power were about me, wholly friendly, and I knew without the shadow of a doubt that at the back of this strife was sheer goodness and, that though this did not imply immunity from danger or death, these things somehow were insignificant and irrelevant . . . .It didn't seem to matter what happened. It was all right beyond.[7]

He was under control, but not his own.

We fly out of control when we forget who we are and where we are supposed to be going. We can become so fascinated with the features of our temporary vehicle we lose sight of the ultimate. The body has a little thirst, so we assuage it. It feels a little lustful, so we satisfy it. The psyche is starved for applause, so we play to the galleries. Our will to dominate itches, so we make another power move. And so it goes, until before we know it, we're spinning out of control yet giving the appearance of controlling everything. Or, in Paul's language, we've become slaves to what is destroying us.

The results? Suicide, depression, withdrawal from people, hiding out, playing the hypocrite, monotonously doing what's expected, hitting the skids. Dying.

It's not too late. We can still take control – by giving it up. The "magic" words are, "God, help me. You take control. I'm ready to serve you. I've been a slave to a different master long enough."

Those who belong to Christ Jesus have crucified the sinful

168

nature with its passions and desires (Gal 5:24).

The fruit of the Spirit is . . . *self-control.*

FOR YOUR FURTHER CONSIDERATION

1. What does self-control mean, in the way the Apostle Paul employs the word?

2. The author says "freedom from authority" is not an option available to us. Why?

3. Why isn't total human autonomy possible?

4. How can we find an adequate compromise between God's way and Satan's way?

5. What was wrong with Mickey Davis' desire to open his old night club as a revival center?

6. How does our knowing our citizenship is in heaven help us to live a more self-controlled life on earth?

7. Explain how taking control by giving up actually works. How has it worked in your life?

Endnotes

1. Tip O'Neill, with William Novak, *Man of the House.* New York: Random House, 1987, p. 15.

2. *Maharani of Maipur,* quoted in *Time,* June 9, 1986, p. 62.

3. Richard Halverson, *Man to Man.* Los Angeles: Cowman Publishing Company, 1961, p. 173.

4. Hallmark Cards, copyrighted.

5. "Born-again club owner returns to strip shows," Paige St. John, The Associated Press. *Mesa Tribune,* February 11, 1987.

6. Elton Trueblood, *The Common Ventures of Life.* Waco: Word Books, 1949, p. 102.

7. Leslie Weatherhead, *Prescription for Anxiety.* London: Hodder and Stoughton, 1956, pp. 132, 133.